FOREWORD BY

THE PEOPLE-MAGNET CHURCH

Attracting Your Community to Christ

COLLEGE PRESS PUBLISHING COMPANY

Joplin, Missouri

College Press Publishing Company
On the web at www.collegepress.com
Toll-free order line 1-800-289-3300

Printed and Bound in the
United States of America

Cover Design by Brett Lyerla

Library of Congress Cataloging-in-Publication Data

Walter, Darren, 1972–
The people-magnet church: attracting your community to Christ/Darren Walter.
p. cm.
Includes bibliographical references.
ISBN 0-89900-872-0 (pbk.)
1. Church growth. I. Title.
BV652.25 W35 2001
254—dc21

2001032524

Dedication

This book is dedicated to all the people
through whom God has made my life so rich,
and to the memory of Kay Bernard
who made everyone feel right at home
and strangers feel like friends.

Acknowledgments

Thank you God for drawing sinners like me
to your side.
Thank you for running after me when I am stubborn
and persistent in my disobedience.
Thank you for extending the invitation to me.
Thank you for warmly welcoming me into your family.

Thank you, Amanda, my awesome wife.
God blessed me with more than I ever thought possible
through your love.
I can't wait to spend the rest of my life with you.
You are a dream builder, a dream supporter,
a dream encourager and a dream come true.
I love you.

Thank you to Dad, Mom, & Kara, to Rich and Gail,
and to the rest of my wonderful family.
Your support is so appreciated.
Thank you to a long list of the best friends in the world.
Special thanks to Scott Tucker, Rob Harris,
Todd Keene, Barbara Hall,
Fritz Kaufman, Debbie Carper, and Mike Chapman.

Foreword

I was delighted when Darren Walter, one of Southeast Christian Church's most beloved staff members, asked me to review his new book, *The People-Magnet Church*. Considering Darren's creativity and people skills, I knew I would be in for a treat! I was not disappointed. Darren is known for his unique ways of making others feel loved and welcomed. He has given Appreciation Dinners for his volunteers with various themes and much variety. "You Shine Like Stars" had an Academy Award theme. Darren, dressed in a tuxedo, greeted each volunteer who entered on a red carpet. The "Golden Smiley Awards" were given to outstanding volunteers at this dinner event. On another occasion, the Guest Services Staff led by Darren loaded up a cart with cookies and other treats and went all over the church building playing kazoos and just basically brightening each employee's day. (You can see why he is so loved by the staff!)

Darren does an outstanding job with one of the largest departments at Southeast Christian Church. After every event we have here, from our Easter Pageant and weekend worship services to our Leadership Conference, I am in awe of the positive comments about our Guest Services volunteers. People who visit are amazed that we have so many "servants' hearts" around here and a great part of that can be attributed to Darren's ministry.

Upon reading *The People-Magnet Church*, I find practical ideas with a personal touch for assisting any church to know how to break down the barriers between visitors and whatever their expectations may be. Involve your entire congregation in this ministry and make your church a place to which you can be proud you invited a guest. Darren helps us to put on "Guest-Colored" glasses to evaluate where a ministry excels as well as where it falls short. His personal research lends a hand in assisting a ministry to be "visitor-friendly," because we should never underestimate the power of a first impression. Prepare to have your toes stepped on periodically—Darren presents a vivid mental picture of where many churches are lacking. But, for now, sit back and enjoy the ride.

Bob Russell, Senior Minister
Southeast Christian Church
Louisville, Kentucky

Table of Contents

Contents

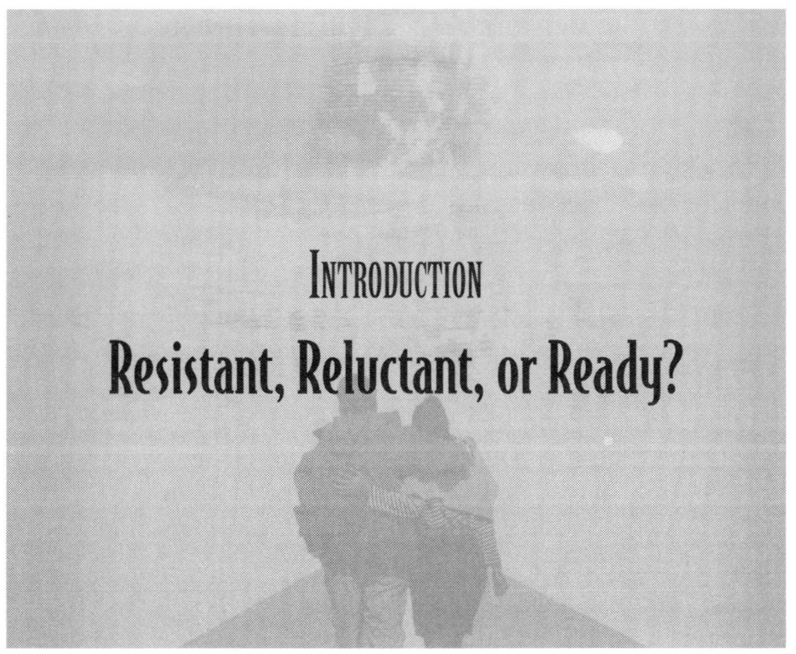

Introduction

Resistant, Reluctant, or Ready?

Take a journey with me to a seaside dock in Joppa. There, a man approaches the ticket counter. "One way ticket to Tarshish please." In my imagination I picture God changing that word "Tarshish" as it travels from the sailor's mouth to the clerk's ear. Then I imagine the clerk's response, "One way ticket to Nineveh, that'll be forty-five dollars and twenty-three cents, sir."

"No, I said, Tarshish. Tar-shish!"
"Sorry sir, I was sure you said Nineveh."
"Nope, I'm headed the opposite direction. Tarshish it is."
"Okay, sir, that'll cost you a little more . . ."

It sure did, didn't it? Jonah wasn't simply *hesitant* to do what God had asked of him; he was *resistant*. God gave him specific instructions to go to Nineveh, and he chose not to. He ignored God's request and hopped a boat to Tarshish. As

Jonah left the ticket counter and walked down the dock, I picture the ship bound for Nineveh docked right beside the one headed to Tarshish. Perhaps they were back to back. I see the Nineveh sign and the Tarshish sign hanging side by side over the boarding area. There's Jonah staring at both signs and both boats and standing right there, smack-dab in the middle of the moment of decision.

You and I have been there too, haven't we? God says, "Go here, say this, do that . . . ." and sometimes we gladly say yes and sometimes we get on the boat headed in the opposite direction. It happens in our personal lives and in the lives of our churches. God makes His request known and it's ignored. God charts out a course for us, and we think we can chart a better course on our own. God maps out the direction our church ought to go and a committee decides to draw up a different map altogether.

As the other passengers boarded the S.S. Tarshish that day and the boat rocked back and forth, I wonder if Jonah's conscience rocked back and forth. One minute trying to convince himself he had done the only thing he could do and the next wanting to get off that boat as fast as he could and be obedient to God and go to Nineveh.

> **God charts out a course for us, and we think we can chart a better course on our own.**

We all know Jonah decided to stay on the boat headed in the opposite direction from God's mission. He remained resistant. The final boarding call was made, and the ship left the port. It's funny how, when you run from God, it never feels like you've run far enough. In a final effort to remove himself from the situation, Jonah ran below deck and took a nap. Jonah's resistance, however, was soon met with a reminder. "Wake up! Call on your god! Maybe he will spare our lives!" The ship was about to be smashed into toothpicks by a sudden storm. The Bible says that Jonah had already told the sailors that he was running from his God. It didn't take long for them to put two and two together. They asked Jonah an important question, "What have you done?" I can't help but think that the sailors' question must have sloshed around in Jonah's mind for a moment. "What have I done?" "Why am I on this boat?" "Why did I disobey God?"

After some discussion between crashing waves, they took Jonah's suggestion and threw him overboard. Jonah went from a nap in the bottom of a gently rocking boat to a fight for his life in a raging sea. But God was nowhere close to being finished with Jonah. Like so many times, God's intervention was also a rescue. This time it was in the form of an extra large fish. God was speaking to Jonah, no doubt about it. "If you won't go to Nineveh, I'll take you there myself." Three days and several prayers later, Jonah hits the sand with a new outlook on life. This time he obeyed God and went to Nineveh.

Like so many times, God's intervention was also a rescue.

On his first day in town Jonah began to proclaim, "Forty more days and Nineveh will be overturned!" The Bible says that all of Nineveh, from the greatest to the least, repented. Amazing. Can you imagine what that must have been like? I would fully expect the story to go in the opposite direction. How ironic in comparison with Jonah's flight from Nineveh! I would expect the city to ignore one man with a doom and gloom message of destruction, but they didn't. The entire city repented. If there's anything the book of Jonah teaches us, it's that God doesn't need talented, "superpeople" to accomplish His will. God used Jonah's resistance and reluctance to do some awesome things. I think there are some applications to be made to our personal lives and the lives of our churches.

The first lesson is that God used Jonah's resistance to change a boatful of lives. Jonah heard God's instructions and took a 180-degree turn in the opposite direction. Even in the midst of Jonah's resistance, God drew a boat full of men to belief in Him. Those shipmates of Jonah didn't know what they were getting themselves into that day when they waved goodbye to the Joppa shoreline. They were enrolled in a crash course in "God's Power 101." After they sent Jonah flying over the side of the ship, the seas became instantly calm. Jonah 1:16 says, "At this the men greatly feared the LORD, and they offered a sacrifice to the LORD and made vows to him." In the middle of Jonah's retreat from his mission, God affects the lives of that ship's crew. Isn't it amazing that God can use anything and anyone to bring Him glory? God uses my life to encourage others even when I don't think I'm being particularly encouraging and when my heart is far from right. God uses you at times when you aren't even aware. Churches are used by God to reach the lost, even when those churches aren't focused on reaching the lost. God uses halfhearted efforts to change hearts. God can use our disobedience to prod others to obey.

Isn't it amazing that God can use anything and anyone to bring Him glory?

The second lesson is similar. God used Jonah's reluctance to change an entire city full of sinful men and women. The Bible doesn't say that Jonah held a month-long crusade or that he bathed his visit to Nineveh in prayer (he had been bathed enough). There was nothing special about Jonah's announcement to the city of Nineveh. He simply said, perhaps with reluctance, "Forty more days and Nineveh will be destroyed." He never gave an invitation. He didn't teach people what repentance was all about. He didn't counsel with a soul. He belted out a simple fact. It was through God's power that the people of that great city from peasant to president repented of their wicked ways and turned to God. Astounding! God took what I would unknowingly judge as Jonah's reluctant, somewhat sad attempt to save the city and turned it into one big altar call where every person responded to God and begged His forgiveness and mercy. WOW! God used Jonah's reluctance and turned it into a revival.

I'm ashamed of how many times I've been reluctant to visit someone, go to a hospital or nursing home, or spend time serving someone, only to have God turn it into a blessing. Maybe God figures my reluctance is what He usually has to work with so He may as well make the best of it. I know I'm reluctant to obey God. I'm guessing you are sometimes reluctant to obey Him as well. I also know that churches are reluctant to obey because churches are made up of people just like you and me. In countless churches everywhere, service is given reluctantly on a regular basis, but I dare say on an equally regular basis the service rendered is used by God to bring glory to His wonderful name whether given in willingness or reluctance.

"So what does Jonah's resistance and reluctance have to do with **my** desire for the church where I volunteer or minister to reach out into the community and attract people to Jesus Christ?" The answer is "A whole lot!"

If God can reach a group of rough sailors in the midst of Jonah's resistance,
if God can bring an entire city to their knees through one reluctant prophet's shouted call to repentance,
what could He do through you and your church if you are truly *ready* to be used by Him to reach your community?

What could God do through a congregation of people who are bursting with eagerness to change their town in the name of Christ? If He uses the resistant and reluctant, what awesome adventures are in store for those who are ready? Are you ready to see what God will do in your life? How about in your church? In your community? What awesome things does God have waiting for those who boldly step aboard the ship bound for Nineveh? What will He do through those who run *after* Him instead of from Him? What will God accomplish through ready people willing to obey? Come aboard and set sail for the destination God has chosen for your church. Help clear the course for those who have never known Him as Captain of their lives.

If God uses the resistant and reluctant, what is in store for the ready?

Lift up the cross like a mighty mast and watch people be drawn to Christ by His magnetic love, truth, and grace.

Chapter 1

Three "M" Words That Make a World of Difference

Square One for The People-Magnet Church

As you begin the journey of becoming a people-magnet church, it's necessary that you understand the difference between three "M" words and how they relate to one another. When the definitions of these words become cloudy or when one word is mistaken for another, there is sure to be trouble. Many churches have difficulty with the most basic directives because of the confusion that surrounds these important words—"message," "methods," and "mission."

The Message

The message to which we're referring is the gospel message. It is the true account of God's demonstration of love for mankind. God sent His Son Jesus to seek and save the lost. He was born of the Virgin Mary and born to die. He lived a sinless life even though He lived through the temptations everyone faces. He healed the sick and lame and healed the wounds of the soul. He turned water to wine and walked on water. He raised the dead and raised the spirits of the people oppressed by legalistic religious rules. He was nailed to the cross, and our sins were nailed there with Him. He died and was taken down. Our sin stayed there. He was buried in a borrowed tomb on land and buried our sin in the depths of the sea. He was resurrected from the dead, and He resurrected hope for life beyond the grave. He was taken up into heaven, and He will take up with Him those who believe when He returns a second time. That's the simple gospel message.

I would imagine and hope that everyone reading this book would agree that the message of the gospel ought not be tampered with or changed. Its truth is timeless and applicable in any age, among any people, within the realm of any culture. The message we preach from our pulpits, teach in our classrooms, and share around our dinner tables, hospital bedsides, and campfires must never change.

The message of the gospel ought not be tampered with or changed.

During a Sunday evening service a church on the West Coast had to evacuate their building because an earthquake struck the area. Thankfully, the earthquake was not severe and the churchgoers were delighted that their building was not harmed. They poured over every square inch of the facility and never found the first crack or sign of damage. Still, the leaders decided they would have the building inspected before resuming normal activity, just to be safe. The inspectors discovered a shocking reality. Even though the building looked fine and there were no visible damages, the officials informed the church body that the building had moved from its foundation, and it would inevitably collapse. They had no other choice but to condemn the building. When the church moves off of the foundation of its message, God's Word, it may *look* secure, but it will inevitably collapse. The message is the heartbeat of what we do and who we are. The Bible is the foundation on which we build our faith, our practices, and our very lives. The message must remain unchanged.

The Method

The methods, on the other hand, are the vehicles that we use to move the message. Our methods are how we communicate the message to our community and culture. One good way to remember the difference between the message and the methods is to keep in mind that the message is singular, but there are many methods. Methods are how we package and deliver the gift of the message.

Methods change over time. Different methods work in communicating the message to different people. A successful method in your hometown may fall flat on its face in someone else's suburb. Methods that worked fifty years ago simply aren't as effective today, and today's methods will fall miserably short ten years from now.

Going door-to-door with information about your church may be the most effective outreach in your community, but in another church's neighborhood it could result in nothing but slammed doors and angry people. On the other hand, a mass mailing cleverly describing your church may work great in that same community where door-to-door visits were a bomb. So, methods must change. The methods your church uses to communicate the gospel message have to change based on the place, time, and situation in which you find yourself.

If we conducted an investigation in our churches today, we would find some churches where it is easier to change the message itself than the methods the church has held onto for years. In some churches today, fewer people would be upset with discarding a section of Scripture than if they heard that the leaders decided to run an ad on the hard rock radio station

When we elevate the methods to the same level or above the level of the message, serious problems result.

in town. When we elevate the methods to the same level or above the level of the message, serious problems result.

No one puts this question in perspective like the Apostle Paul. In 1 Corinthians 9:19-23 Paul wrote

> *Though I am free and belong to no man, I make myself a slave to everyone, to win as many as possible. To the Jews I became like a Jew, to win the Jews. To those under the law I became like one under the law (though I myself am not under the law), so as to win those under the law. To those not having the law I became like one not having the law (though I am not free from God's law but am under Christ's law), so as to win those not having the law. To the weak I became weak, to win the weak. I have become all things to all men so that by all possible means I might save some. I do all this for the sake of the gospel.*

In this powerful section of Scripture, Paul shows us that he is willing to set aside everything but the message itself to win the lost. Due to Paul's background of being under the law, I would think he would be so in love with living under grace that he would shy away from even the thought of returning to that mind-set for any reason, but he didn't. He loved the people under the law more than he loved his freedom. His next example is the kicker for me. Paul says that even though he was bound by the law of Christ, he became like those not having law. He became like the people you and I see every day—not bound by God's law, not under the grace of Jesus Christ. He became like those who didn't know God's law to win them over to that law of love. To the weak, those without hope, those without strength and purpose, he became weak. Why? To win the weak.

Paul is willing to change his method of reaching people based on those he's trying to reach. When we take the time to use new and innovative methods to reach the lost, we demonstrate our love for the message. That's how Paul closes his thought. *"I have become all things to all men so that by all possible means I might save some. I do all this for the sake of the gospel."* He tells us that he has tried all kinds of methods to reach all kinds of people, so that in any way possible, he might save people and bring them to a relationship with

Christ. Then he explains why, *"For the sake of the gospel."* He does all of this because of the unchanging message! The power of God's message, the gospel, compels him to reach out to people using whatever method will be most effective.

How different would our churches be today if we concerned ourselves with following Paul's example? What if we made it our business to identify with people outside of Christ? To go where they go? To meet them on their terms? The fact of the matter is, it is the church's business to do just that! At what point did we turn everything upside down and say to the world, "You have to spend time on our turf and talk like us and dress like us and act like us before we'll accept you!" By silently turning their backs to the church, much of the world is saying to us, "You have to spend time on *our* turf, talk like *us*, dress like *us*, and not be embarrassed to be seen with *us*, before our hearts will accept your message and your Jesus."

Paul began with this statement, *"Though I am free and belong to no man, I make myself a slave to everyone, to win as many as possible"* When was the last time the church considered itself a slave to those who don't know Christ? Chain your church to your community. Handcuff your church to your culture. Become the slave of those who don't know Christ and don't care to know Him . . . yet.

When was the last time the church considered itself a slave to those who don't know Christ?

The church is not "OF" this world. We see differently, think differently, and have a different purpose and direction. The church serves a different Master, and we are set apart to carry out the will of our Father. But the church must never forget that we are "IN" the world. God has placed us in the society and culture we find ourselves in, not by accident but on purpose, and that purpose is to infiltrate, influence, and impact the world that surrounds us.

To use the excuse that we ought not reach out to the world because the world and its ways might rub off on us is a pathetic excuse, a blindness to the Scripture, and nothing more than a not-so-clever way to disguise our disobedience. Years ago I sat in my apartment one Sunday morning before church. I listened in disbelief to a television preacher as he explained why he needed his own personal jet. Funny, the fact that he had his own jet wasn't what was so appalling. The thing I found disturbing was his reasoning behind the purchase. He explained to his congregation that he was "anointed by God" and that he spent much of his time flying all over the country preaching the message of God. He simply could not risk being seated by a sinner on a commercial flight. "I can't have their sin rubbing off on me," he said. "I am sanctified. I am set apart. I am anointed by God." With everything in me I wanted to jump through my TV set and into the auditorium where he was "preaching" and remind him that he was sanctified, set apart, and anointed by God for one purpose. That purpose was to get his sanctified hands dirty ministering to people. That purpose was to place his set-apart self in the middle of people who need God. That purpose was to share his anointing with the lost people on the commercial flight. The very same people that he was too good to sit by or be on the same plane with.

The church is not sanctified to become sanctuary-fied, locking its members away from a lost world. The church is not set apart to *stay apart* from the culture in which it has been placed. The anointed message was not anointed to be shared and passed back and forth from believer to believer but to be shared anew with those who've never heard it.

If we choose not to follow Paul's example, then we ought to follow God's example. God in His wisdom and love for us made some amazing decisions. God decided to meet us on our terms. He decided to dress as we do. He decided to talk as we talk. He decided to live as we live. He decided to become one of us. God knew that a simple announcement, "Please join me in Heaven," would not get the job done. God knew that if we could not relate to Him, we would not accept Him. God knew that if we could not see His love, we would not believe His love. God knew that if we could not touch His skin, He could not touch our hearts. So He sent

Jesus—Emmanuel, God with us. Jesus was sanctified, set apart and anointed, but He rubbed shoulders with those who were not. Matthew 11:19 reminds us that Jesus was accused of being a glutton and a drunkard because He was a friend to tax collectors and sinners. He got His hands dirty serving those who did not deserve to be served. He got His hands bloody loving those who did not deserve love.

God knew that if we could not touch His skin, He could not touch our hearts.

God sent Jesus to build a cross-shaped bridge between Him and a dying world. Now, God is sending us to build a bridge to a dying world. Are we willing to change our methods in order to relate to the people we are trying to reach, or must they come to Christ on *our* terms? Are we so afraid of becoming tainted by the world that we never reach out to it? Will we stay in our private jets—the ones with steeples and crosses on top? We are called to mix and mingle in this world and rub off on it. We are called to weave the message in and out of our daily contacts with our culture. We are called to communicate the timeless, unchanging message to an ever-changing society that is running out of time. But there is one more "M" word . . .

The Mission

Your church can serve many purposes in the community and in the lives of your members and regulars, but everything your church does must be able to be reduced to a basic mission. A lot has been written and discussed on the subject of "mission statements" both in the business world and in the church realm, and there's no secret why. The mission you discover and articulate to the people that make up your church will become the driving force for all you do. It will define who you are and why you exist. I am certainly no expert on how to write a mission statement for your church, so I'll spend my time on the underlying concept that should support whatever final mission and mission statement you choose.

Three "M" Words

We'll talk a great deal in this book about *first impressions*. Let's take a moment now and talk about the most important last impression ever given. In Matthew 28:18-20 Jesus gives a final direction to His followers. It's known as the Great Commission because it is Christ's final directive to those on earth who bear His name. Before He left them wide-eyed and slack-jawed, He said this:

> *All authority in heaven and on earth has been given to me. Therefore go and make disciples of all nations, baptizing them in the name of the Father and of the Son and of the Holy Spirit, and teaching them to obey everything I have commanded you. And surely I am with you always, to the very end of the age.*

Jesus' mission is for the church to go into the world and make disciples of everyone. Then Jesus explains the basics of how that should be done, by baptizing them in the name of the Father, Son, and Holy Spirit, and by teaching them to obey His commands. But notice Jesus never takes the time to get specific with methods. Why? Because methods change. From flannelgraph to charts and graphs, from door-to-door to direct mail, from confrontation to commercials, from shelter for the homeless to house churches, methods change and must. Your church's mission lies somewhere between the message and the methods.

The Mission of the church is where the message and the methods come together.

The Mission of the church is where the message and the methods come together. Jesus told His disciples to take the message into the world, to baptize and teach. How your church accomplishes that commission will be what sets you apart and what magnetically attracts the people of your particular city or community or village to your church and ultimately to Christ. *How* churches reach out will change from church to church. *Why* churches reach out should be the same. We reach out to people around us because the message of God's Word is true and because we know God's power to change their lives for eternity travels through the truth of His message.

When the unchanging, life-changing message of the gospel is united with a creative, tailor-made method of communicating the message to the people you want to reach, there's no limit to what God can and will do. Place the timeless message and a cutting-edge method in the hands of your church people and look out! People with a mission like that are hard to hold back or discourage! The simple equation of message + method = mission will cut down on division and increase multiplication in your ministry. These three words are the foundation of becoming a people-magnet church. If we only have the message and no method to communicate it effectively, our congregations will preach and teach and share among themselves—alone. If we have a snappy new method but compromise on the message, God will not bless our efforts and we are deceiving others and ourselves and will be judged accordingly. But if we combine the exciting message of the gospel with an up-to-date method, our fellow disciples will be ignited with mission and purpose. And with God's help we can change the world for Christ and change eternity for the world.

Chapter 2

Don't Rest on Your Imaginary Laurels

The Role That Perception Plays in Your Church's Magnetism

Let's say your boss calls you into his office and says, "You've done such a good job lately, I have something special for you." Your perception of that event will cause you to think or react in one of several different ways. Does your boss have a gift he'd like to give you to show his appreciation of your efforts, maybe a gift certificate to a nice restaurant? Or, maybe he's been so impressed with you lately that he isn't giving you a gift at all; he's giving you a very difficult assignment that nobody else wants to handle.

How a person perceives a situation will govern how he reacts to that situation. Your reaction to other people when you think you are contributing to the humor of a conversation with friends is very different compared with how you react when you perceive you are being made fun of.

Many times we develop a perception about a person before we ever meet that person, or we develop a perception about an event without ever experiencing the event ourselves. Spouses, coworkers, fellow church leaders, or people you overhear in the line at the grocery store can give you a perception overhaul, completely changing your opinion.

> "You're not going to like the new supervisor. I heard she is overbearing, mean, and unreasonable!"
>
> "This movie may be a little slow, but if you just bear with it, the last five minutes are really good."
>
> "I've heard so many good things about this new toothpaste; several of my friends said that they will never go back to their old brand."

We're open to all kinds of thoughts and ideas, and we often allow them to shape what we think and how we feel about things.

It's as if our mind is a big suggestion box. We're open to all kinds of thoughts and ideas, and we often allow them to shape what we think and how we feel about things.

Time for a Reality Check

Perception is a powerful thing. Some even go so far as to say perception is reality. In many cases that's true. If I perceive that the new supervisor is impossible to deal with, unreasonable, and a downright difficult person, I will act accordingly. I might approach the new supervisor with a great deal of caution. I may become anxious and nervous about talking to her or discussing problems with her. I certainly would avoid her office. My actions reflect my perception. But what if my perception of the new supervisor is all wrong? What if the truth is that she is a very kind, gracious person and easy to work with? Until my false perception is changed over time, it makes no difference. I still operate as if my perception were reality. In my mind it *is* reality.

So the inevitable question is posed, "How do people in your community perceive your church?" Do they perceive your church as active, alive, and growing, or unfriendly, cold, and standoffish? Remember, if the perception is that your church is "unwelcoming" to guests, it doesn't really matter if that's a true assessment or not. Those who perceive it that way will act accordingly. Why would I try a church that I perceive to be not caring about my family's needs? Why would I want to go through the trouble of going to church if I perceive it as unfriendly or cliquish? The answer is, I wouldn't. The important first step to take toward assuring that your church is seen in a true and good light is to determine exactly what perceptions of your church exist in your community.

Determine what perceptions of your church exist in your community.

Going on a Perception Hunt

How would you go about finding out what the community's perception of your church is? Well, you could form a committee of church members and ask them what they think. But then again, if you want to know what the community thinks, who cares what a committee of church people say? You are interested in the perceptions and thoughts of people in your town who have never been to your church. Their perspective on church is the gold mine you've been searching for. Discover their opinions of church and their personal thoughts about your church, and you will have uncovered a priceless fortune! When you begin digging around for the community's perception, you can't ask yourself or church leaders or church regulars what they think your community is thinking. The most effective approach may be (surprise!) to actually *ask* the community what they think of your church! Until you begin this quest for priceless perspective, the task will seem pretty daunting. The key is to jump in headfirst. The worst thing that could happen is the people you approach will not answer your questions and will walk off; they may even give you an earful about this "church stuff." Great! If they're that ticked off at church and you got a chance to hear their feelings, thank God and devote yourself to reaching people with that opinion. However, if you approach people with graciousness and politeness, most will respond in like manner and will be honest with you about their perceptions of church. Imagine what kind of valuable information you will uncover by asking people about their thoughts on church, why they go or don't go, what the ideal church would be like, and if they have any particular thoughts or perceptions about your church.

The local grocery store, laundry facility, or area shopping mall are obvious locations for beginning this challenge. However, it can also be as simple as interviewing acquaintances in your office. How about the parent sitting next to you at ball practice? What a great way to pass the time while you wait.

Begin by introducing yourself and asking if they have about a minute to answer a few simple questions. If they do not have time to talk, simply thank them and keep moving. It also helps if you're dressed nicely, have a nametag and a clipboard and have fresh breath and a sincere smile. Your search could begin with casual discussions with people you've never met before at the grocery store. You could go house to house taking a survey of a particular neighborhood. Ask a local company or business if you can bring donuts and coffee to their employees and ask them questions about church and their family's needs. Develop a relationship with a movie theater or restaurant and purchase "One Dollar Off" coupons from them to hand out to people who will take time to answer your questions. (Always get permission and operate "aboveboard" while you're digging around for perceptions and opinions.) There are lots of ways to gather and uncover the data on the area's perception of your church. The important thing is that you ask, listen, and respond in some way. If you find particularly receptive people, have something prepared for them about your church or ask if you may have their permission to send them information on your church. Give a small gift to those who answer your questions. Make it a brief, positive, and relational situation. What a great oppor-

You could begin with casual discussions at the grocery store.

tunity to build a positive reputation of your church while you gather information from your community!

Bridge over the Perception River

We've learned that, like the water that flows in a river, a person's perception of your church is fluid. It can change based on what seems to be an insignificant fact. The water in a river glides around rocks and driftwood, splashing from side to side and bouncing its way around bends. Similarly a person's perception can be tossed from one side of the spectrum to another based on the comment of a friend, a personal observation, or based on how the outside of your facility appears. Your goal is to build a bridge over those tossing waves of perception giving the people of your community the means to walk across to the other side on solid facts. There are several planks in that bridge. Let's discuss the step-by-step trek of an unchurched person as she makes her way across the waters of perception to a clearer understanding of your church.

The first plank in the bridge is the starting point—the community's current perception of your church. You'll find what those current perceptions are after your information-gathering mission through your community is complete. After the formal or informal surveys are complete, gather the people together who helped you survey your community and review and discuss what you learned. Discuss any recurring themes or thoughts that surfaced during your interviews with the people of your town. Did most of the people you talked with indicate they attend church on a regular basis or did most not attend a church regularly? Analyze their responses as to why they attend a church and dissect the responses of those who explained why they do not attend church. What specific characteristics did they mention would make up the ideal church? What are the needs of their families? Have they ever heard of your church? What do they know about it?

You could find good or bad perceptions or no perception at all.

What are their perceptions? You may find your church is perceived very well in the community, or you may find that there's a negative perception or none at all. No matter what the outcome, don't be discouraged. You now have information on which you can build.

Plank number two is to decide what kind of church you want to be. You want people's perception of your church to be a true perception no doubt, but what does that look like? How do you want the people in your town or city to perceive Christ's church? Deciding what kind of church you want to be seems like a simple task, but it is stuffed full of questions to ponder and answer among team members. In my limited experience I've seen many churches with this root problem. They don't know what kind of church they want to be. They are in limbo between the church they used to be and dreams of the kind of church they would like to become.

Take, for example, First Church of We're Not Sure. About 30% of First Church's members want it to be the church it used to be. They recall dinner on the grounds, hymn sings on Sunday night, and a facility and a message that was simple and straightforward. That dedicated 30% react vocally against the 50% that want First Church to be the church of the new millennium. They'd like to exchange dinners on the grounds for a coffee shop in the fellowship hall. An occasional hymn is okay but they prefer an upbeat worship time, and Sunday nights are nonexistent in their perception of the futuristic First Church. They dream of an updated, fresh facility with a gymnasium and walking track, and the more illustrations and object lessons you can use in communicating the message the better! What about the other 20% of the people? They're either somewhere between the two, or they're waiting to see how First Church's identity crisis pans out so they can either make themselves at home or hit the road. The truth is it's very difficult, if not impossible, to please both groups of people. Somewhere along the line the leaders of First Church have to decide what kind of church they're going to be. I'm speaking of going beyond the important foundation of the message itself. I'm talking about the style the church adopts. Will First

Church be the "Family Church" in town or maybe the "Traditional Church"? Will they become the "Contemporary, Cutting-Edge Church"? What do they want to be known for in their community? The answer to that question will determine their direction as a church. The answer to that question will let them know the type of people they will target to reach with the gospel. The answer to that question will outline the task ahead in changing their town's perception of Christ's church.

The answer to the question of what you want to be known for will determine the direction you take.

The third plank is showing the community what kind of church you are. This third plank in the bridge and all subsequent planks reflect the church's identity and make several statements to the community forming their evolving perception of the church. Let's say that First Church decided that they were going to become the "Family Church" in town. They felt God's leading to reach out to and minister to families in their city. They want to be known in their area as the church where families really grow and are nurtured and encouraged. They realize that the term "family" could encompass everyone from a one-day-old infant to someone who just celebrated his one hundred and first birthday, but they've chosen to begin with their ministry focus on young families in their community. The first questions they should ask themselves are, "What would a church known as the 'Family Church' in town look like? What ministries would they provide? How would they reach out into the community? How would such a focus reflect on their facilities, their worship, their opportunities for fellowship?" You could make a long list right now of the kinds of things in which a "Family Church" would be involved. They might offer an outrageously fun after-school program for kids. How about ministries that reach out to families in trouble? A practical sermon series on improving your marriage, seminars on how to parent difficult teens, a small group for mothers of infants, "Parent's Night Out" programs, and more would all be typical of the kinds of activities and services available. First

Church could make a mile-long list of such ministries that would reach out to people and communicate to everyone: "We are the family church in town!"

By being intentional about the type of church you want to be, you'll communicate your passion to the world around you, and God will draw people to your church with matching needs and matching passions. As you build your bridge over the perception river, you'll see your community moving from a nonexistent or negative perception of your church to a positive and accurate perception, step by step. Perception *is* reality. You have the ability with God's blessing, creativity, and power to recreate your church's style. In so doing, your church attracts specific people to that newly created context in which they will experience God's message of love, truth, and grace for their lives.

By being intentional about the type of church you want to be, you'll communicate your passion to the world around you.

Chapter 3

A Sheep in Guest's Clothing

The Value of Outside Perspective

One of my favorite parts in my ministry is the opportunity to present the "People Magnet Seminar" to churches in their own environment. Occasionally church leaders will ask me to attend their church on a Sunday morning as an unannounced observer, and later that day or evening I will present the seminar and tell the people of the church my observations from being among them that morning. Did I feel welcomed and at home as a newcomer? Were the entrances and parking areas easy to negotiate? Were signs easy to read and follow? Was I greeted warmly? What are my impressions of their facility? Basically, if I were a guest, would I want to come back for a second visit?

This kind of information can be very helpful to your church. After we become familiar with a program, our surroundings, or the people in those surroundings, we become desensitized. We, in fact, are part of those surroundings our-

We become desensitized to what we are too familiar with.

selves, and therefore it's very difficult for us to stand back and see things with an objective eye. Business owners call this being "store blind." You open the shop day after day and soon you don't notice that "aisle 4" is cluttered or that a certain display makes it inconvenient for people to actually get to the product. You don't notice how apathetic a clerk comes across when he recites the "Have a nice (insert yawn here) day" for the twelve thousandth time. As a result, the business suffers. Churches are no different. If you're like most folks that would be interested in this book, you've been an active part of your church for some time, maybe even twenty years or more. After seeing the facility once a week, three or four times a week, or if you're on the ministry staff, every single day, it's easy to become blind to all that's around you. You stop noticing the dingy corners or the out-of-date restrooms or the frayed carpet. Gaining an outside perspective can make all the difference to your church. It can be an eye-opening experience!

An "undercover" church visit is not only eye opening to your church, but I can assure you it's been pretty eye opening for me, too. Allow me to share a few stories with you that will illustrate the importance of outside perspective. Being "a sheep in guest's clothing" has taught me a lot about what guests must feel like when they visit our churches for the first time. The churches described below have been given aliases and I've combined events from several churches into a couple of stories to protect the friendly and the not so friendly.

Alone in a Crowd

I remember visiting a small church one Sunday morning. It so happened that my wife, Amanda, could not go with me, so I was by myself. I approached the church and noticed two separate driveways and three separate entrances, any of which could have been the front door of choice for the regular churchgoers. At first glance I had no idea where to go. I found a place to park and followed a few people into the building. No one spoke to me on the way in. Let me say before we venture any further that I grew up in church. I can't think of a place where I'm more comfortable, yet I felt nervous and apprehensive walking into a church by myself not knowing a soul inside. That was a feeling I don't ever want to forget. As I made my way under the covered drive and up to the door, several gentlemen were standing outside talking. Again, no one said anything to me. I was greeted just inside the door by a gentleman who handed me a bulletin and plainly said, "Good morning." I returned the greeting and walked into the lobby area. A very nice woman wished me a cheery and sincere, "Good morning, sir!" I was instantly relieved.

I said, "This is my first time here, would you be able to tell me where your restrooms are located?"

"Sure," she said with a smile. "Dave here will show you right to them. They're kind of hard to find." I was impressed that she sent someone with me to show me right where they were rather than point the way or try to give me directions verbally. Afterward, I made my way into the sanctuary and sat about one third of the way over on an empty pew. I watched as the church filled. No one sat on my pew. No one said good morning to me. It wasn't that the church was dead. There were good mornings bouncing all over the church, but none bounced my way. I watched people joke with one another and laugh and enjoy each other's company, but no one spoke to me. For once in my life, I realized what it must be like to be a first-time guest at a church. It was an awkward feeling. I've been to many churches, but in every case I've either been a regular attendee, with someone I knew, being hosted by someone, or the speaker with whom everyone wanted to speak. I had never been a lonely visitor who had no connections. Then it hit me. Most churches think they are friendly because they are friendly to themselves. If I had interviewed the people in

Most churches think they are friendly because they are friendly to themselves.

that church, I'd bet 90% of them would have told me they thought their church was a friendly church. But that would have been based on how they treat one another, not how they treat a new face. It's worth repeating: *most churches think they are friendly because they are friendly to themselves.* The service was enjoyable, and when it was over I made a beeline for the door. The minister was the only person who spoke to me after my initial two greetings that occurred in the first 60 seconds of my visit.

Joe Saves the Day

During a similar visit, my wife and I were able to go to another church as a team. Amanda has a sanguine personality, which means she is a very fun-loving, extroverted person who enjoys people. Before we arrived at the church, I reminded her that we were playing the role of unchurched guests and that meant we were not responsible for befriending anyone that day. "You can speak if you're spoken to," I coached, "but don't start conversations with people or try to engage them with a smile or a good morning." This was difficult for her, but we got through the morning undetected. I might also add we got through the morning virtually ungreeted as well.

We searched for a parking place and walked in with other folks. We passed by several people who were chatting at the main entrance. As we entered, a lady and her young daughter were stationed at the door. The young girl greeted us but seemed almost frightened to be saying hello to people. We couldn't help but smile, and we returned a polite, "Good morning." We wiggled our way through a sea of people in the lobby area. Just like at the other church, these people were enjoying great Christian fellowship, but no one seemed to notice us. Amanda and I continued through the doorway leading into the sanctuary where a greeter handed us a bulletin, looked me square in the eye, and said noth-

They were enjoying great Christian fellowship, but no one seemed to notice us.

ing. We sat down toward the back of the building. No one spoke to us in the fifteen minutes before the service. Once the service began, the congregation was given a few moments to say hello to everyone seated around them. No one shook our hand during that designated greeting time either. Again, people were friendly to one another but not to the guests. When the service was over, we turned to leave. A kind older lady took a moment to say, "Welcome, we're glad you're here today." She shook hands with us and I cheered inside. "Thank you, Lord! At least one person took the time to say hello to an unfamiliar face here today!" What a great yet simple lesson could be learned from that sweet lady.

But our experience was far from over. We thought we'd give the "Welcome Center" a try. I asked where the restrooms were, and my wife asked where we'd take our two-year-old son if we brought him back with us next time. Okay, so we don't have any children, but we figured that we may one day, and if we came back, we'd want to know where to take him! The woman at the "Welcome Center" was very friendly. You could tell she had a genuine love for people. She answered my restroom question but wasn't exactly sure where we'd go with our two-year-old. She pointed down the hallway to the educational rooms and assured us someone down there would know. She wanted to help; she just hadn't been given good information.

We decided we'd walk down the hallway and look lost to see what might happen. A middle-aged gentleman asked if he could help us. Let's call him Joe. Joe was very friendly and struck up a conversation with us right away. He showed us all around the children's ministry area, told us how much he and his family loved the church, and continued to show interest in us. If I were a leader at that church, I'd put Joe in charge of the hospitality ministry and I'd turn him loose every Sunday to model to all the volunteers how to make guests feel at home.

If I were a leader at that church, I'd put Joe in charge of the hospitality ministry.

What's the Big Deal?

The good news is that because of the blood of Jesus Christ and His sacrifice for me, I'm going to heaven by God's grace, regardless of how people treat me in any church. The bad news is that there are people who do not know God's grace and are unaware of Christ's sacrifice. They are going to Hell. And they will make a decision to accept or reject God based on how they are received in His House, by you and me. I'm not trying to be over dramatic here. I truly believe that eternity hangs in the balance when a guest walks through the doors of your church. Those who volunteer their time to greet, welcome, usher, and answer questions of those visiting have some of the most important challenges in the entire church body. Many times we only have one chance to make an impression, one shot at showing our love for people. Doesn't the ministry of welcome deserve our very best efforts? Shouldn't we pour our time, attention, and passion into developing the people of our churches into people who reach out to the guests on a regular basis? Too little importance has been placed on making guests feel genuinely welcomed in our churches. After spending a few minutes in your facility and with the people of your church, the guest should feel like he's wanted, like we're happy that he's there, and we're anxious to make him a part of what's going on at a pace that is comfortable for him. The fact is most guests make up their minds whether they'll return for a second time in the first few moments of their visit. Long before they hear the sermon or the solos, they've decided if they'll ever come back based on how we treat them.

Many times we only have one chance to make an impression, one shot at showing our love for people.

Is It Happening in Your Church?

Wouldn't you be heartbroken to know that there were guests at your church to whom no one spoke? To think that people are giving church a try, making an effort to check God out, and walking out church doors feeling unwelcomed and out of place brings shame to God's name. Maybe it's happening in your church on a regular basis and you just aren't aware of it.

Do I think people in the churches I visited were intentionally rude to me? Do I think they wanted me to feel unwelcomed and uncomfortable? No. I think some didn't even notice I was there; they haven't been trained to recognize guests. Some noticed but didn't know how to approach me or make me feel welcomed. They were afraid to try, afraid to make the first move. I think some were too busy doing church stuff or talking to church people to take inventory of the people around them and consider if there was anyone who looked new, curious, or uncomfortable.

Asking someone who's not familiar with your church to serve as an undercover guest is a great way to get some valuable feedback. If it's not possible to do that right away, then make an effort to take off your church blinders and really see people this Sunday. If you don't know someone's name or you've never seen that person before, that's your cue to make the first move and introduce yourself. Say good morning. Smile. Welcome her. It won't turn you into a frog, it won't hurt, and it won't cost you anything, but taking the initiative will turn you into a more sensitive Christian. It will make you and the other person feel better. More importantly, not going out of your way to be kind and welcoming could cost your church and God's Kingdom dearly. Let's elevate the quality of our facilities, equip our people with skills to make guests feel at home, and build church communities that view loving, serving, and involving guests as the natural thing to do. It's all a part of making your church one that will *draw* people so that Christ can *draw* them to Himself.

If you don't know someone's name or you've never seen them before, that's your cue to make the first move

Chapter 4

If Looks Could Kill, Would Your Church Still Be Alive?

The Physical Appearance of Your Church Facility

As you read the next few lines slowly, picture yourself in the places listed. Picture them in as much detail as you possibly can. As you think about the place, think about what it looks like, feels like, and smells like. What's the temperature in each room? How does each place make you feel? Imagine yourself in:

> A prison cell . . . a ballroom . . . a courtroom . . . a fast food restaurant . . . a five-star restaurant . . . your favorite easy chair . . . a small country church . . . a warehouse . . . the oval office . . . a factory assembly line . . . an ancient cathedral . . . around the fireplace on Christmas Eve . . . a porch swing on a lazy afternoon.

If you weren't in a hurry to read this chapter and you took your time to think about each of those places, you pictured them vividly in your mind's eye. Each and every place had a different feeling. Some of the rooms were cold and empty while others were warm and inviting. Some were plain and simple, while others were ornate and beautiful. Some elicited respect or felt intimidating and others made you feel like you could stay forever.

Never underestimate the power the look of a room, building, or space can have in shaping your impressions and feelings about that place. The design and aesthetics of a room can communicate a great deal of information. It communicates whether or not you are a welcomed guest or an outsider. A room's look communicates the purpose for that space. It communicates how you are expected to behave while you're there. So the big question is, "What is your church facility communicating to your guests?" If a picture is worth a thousand words, what words are being shouted at your guests when they pay you a visit?

A room's look communicates the purpose for that space.

Now some would argue that the church ought not to be spending time and energy and certainly not tithe money on something as superficial and nonspiritual as carpet, paint, furniture, and the like. People ought to be spiritually mature enough to look past a few burnt out lightbulbs and out-of-date colors! Let's address that before we get down to the nitty-gritty of landscape and lamps. The fact is that stuff like carpet, paint, and furniture is just that—stuff. And all that stuff is guilty as charged. It's nonspiritual stuff. It's superficial, nonessential, "of this world" kind of stuff. Having said all that, it's important to consider a few things. First of all, it's a question of mission versus methods, as we talked about in chapter one. We are not "of the world" but we *are in* it. We must operate in the setting, society, and culture where God has placed us. In fact, He's called us to reach out to that culture, not shy away from it. I doubt anyone would question the fact that physical appearance is important in our society today. But many churches seem to think that people check their culture at the front door. They do not. We do not.

Before we beat up on those nonspiritual types that care about such things, let's consider for a moment our own personal preferences. Let's say you want to do some banking. You pull into the bank's parking lot and notice the shrubbery is unkempt and happens to be taller than your car. You open the door, and there's still a flyer on the glass reminding you the bank will be closed on Christmas Day (it's now spring). You walk in and half of the avocado green tile has been chipped away from wear and tear. The lobby hasn't been cleaned in months. You notice cobwebs on the light fixtures and the walls haven't seen a fresh coat of paint since war bonds were the new thing in town. How would you feel about leaving your money with that bank? You skeptics in the audience are saying, "Yeah, but I've been banking there for years and years." Maybe you started banking there when the bank was new and fresh. Maybe you've developed relationships and in the process of banking there twice a week for the last umpteen years, you've become used to the surroundings, and you don't even notice the tile or the cobwebs or the dingy walls. But you know what? People who visit the bank for the first time notice. People who are shopping for a bank notice. That's why they bank down the street.

So, should people be spiritually mature enough to see past what a church looks like inside and out? Yes, I suppose people should be spiritually mature enough not to care about that, but since when is the church looking for spiritually mature people? I was under the impression that the church existed to seek out those who don't know God. The look of your facility is an important step to your church becoming a people magnet and a magnet to Christ. Right or wrong, physical appearance is one of the many criteria guests will consider when deciding to attend your church for the first time or whether or not they'll return for visit number two.

Since when is the church looking for spiritually mature people?

Getting Started

All ministry is better when there's a team of people working together in that ministry. Guest Services, Hospitality, or whatever creative name you give this ministry makes no difference. Find a group of people that are passionate about attracting guests to your church. Don't think you have to have 10 or 20 people to form this team. I would rather have 2 or 3 people who are passionate and dedicated than 25 who are sort of interested. Another word about the right people: please make sure that there are men *and* women on this team. They both play a crucial role. Often men are involved in improvement projects around the church from a construction or technical aspect. Their expertise is very valuable. However, don't make the mistake of excluding women from this process. Women have a God-given eye for detail. They have a sense about what a welcoming and warm room should look and feel like. Remember, oftentimes mom will be the driving force behind whether her visiting family will ever return to your church. Statistics show mom is the one who encourages the family to come to church. The women on your ministry team share her perspective. Leave women out of your team, and you'll only be a fraction as effective as you could be.

Make sure the hospitality team includes both men and women.

It's a mistake to begin this ministry focus without prayer. Pray separately and pray as a team. Ask God to give you sensitivity to His leading and to the perspective of the guest who doesn't know Him yet. Also, ask God to help you determine priorities. The first stage of this effort will consist of gathering information and thinking of creative ways to make your church more "magnetic." The second stage is determining exactly where to start. Unless you have an unlimited supply of time, money, and committed people, you'll have to prioritize. If your church does have an unlimited supply of time, money, and committed people, please put this book down and give me a call right away.

Putting on Your Guest-Colored Glasses

A great place to begin the process of improving the look of your facilities is to put on your guest-colored glasses. That is, look at your facility as if you were visiting for the first time. Look at things you haven't looked at in a while or things you've overlooked for months or years. You can accomplish this in many different ways. *First*, make a videotape of your walk through. Start outside in the parking lot. Comb over every section of the lot and outside of the building. Look at your church sign, the front door, and the front steps. As you film, make comments about what you notice. The camera will force you to focus on one area or item at a time rather than glancing hurriedly.

A *second* way to accomplish this is to make it a group effort. I suggest maybe 2 or 3 couples for this project. Again, that's important because it's essential that women be included in the process. Make a fun event out of this. I suggest you do the walk-through one afternoon while there's still plenty of daylight. Then go out to dinner together and return to the church and do the same thing after it's dark. Different things will be noticeable during daylight and nighttime hours. If you don't have access to a video camera, buy a few disposable cameras and take plenty of good notes as you go. Do the same inside the building. Look at everything from the carpet to the ceiling.

A *third* way to get a guest's perspective on your facility may be the most effective yet. Find one or more friends who've never been to your church before and ask them to do a walk-through with you. Ask them to point out what they notice and assure them it's better if they don't hold back their true opinion. Maybe using a combination of these options would give you the best results. Odds are you'll have a long list of things on which to get started. Now, let's get specific about the exterior and interior of your facility.

The Great Outdoors

When looking at the exterior appearance of your church building, start by asking, "What does the outside of

If people look at your building and assume that hedge trimmers and paint are against your religious beliefs, it's time for a change.

our building say to the community?" If your building says, "We don't care." Or, "We used to care several years ago," you're obviously sending the wrong message. Does the exterior of your facility say to those who pass by, "Our church isn't current and up to date"? If people look at your building and assume that hedge trimmers and paint are against your religious beliefs, it's time for a change.

What do you want your building and grounds to say to the community? When someone glances in your direction, what impression of your church would you like him to have? A great exterior appearance should say, "We care! This 'church thing' is important to us!" Your facility should *invite* the guest. It should say, "Come on in, we're ready for you." Your goal is to change the topic of conversation inside the cars that go by. Comments like, "Wow! Isn't that lawn beautiful?" or, "That church always looks great no matter what the season," are music to the ears.

Curb Appeal

If you've ever sold a home or done some shopping for a home, you've probably heard the term "Curb Appeal." Curb Appeal is what changes a drive-by-gawker into a potential buyer. The objective is to make your house as appealing from the curb as possible so shoppers will want a closer look at the inside—and maybe become the next homeowner. If I put my house on the market and I was interested in curb appeal, wanting to generate as much interest in my house as possible, the investment of extra cash and care on the exterior of my home makes sense. I might mow the grass on a more regular basis. I would trim the shrubbery and use the weed whacker. I would even go to the trouble of planting some nice flowers out front. That extra effort in making the outside of my house look good may result in getting more people to take a look at the inside.

How many cars drive by your church building in an average 24-hour period? The answer to that question could help you determine how high curb appeal should rate on your list of priorities. Spending some time during rush hour counting cars that pass by your church may make you feel silly, but it could be eye opening. A few outdoor improvements could gain the attention of the passing public and stir the curiosity of the community. How many potential guests pass by your front door every day?

Show Us a Sign, Lord

A quality sign is a big investment, perhaps the largest investment we'll discuss in this chapter. But realize that your church sign may be *the* distinguishing mark that identifies who you are to the community. The sign you select tells not only who you are in terms of identity, "Sunny Oak Church" for example, but it also communicates your church's style. Is your sign traditional with white colonial columns and finials? Is it contemporary with the letters imbedded in an abstract concrete shape? Is it colorful and fun or simple and to the point? Your sign should let people know more than what time your services start. It should give them a hint about the type of church you are.

There are plenty of sign companies, some specializing in church signs, which will walk you step by step through the process. They'll bring valuable expertise to the table by determining where your sign should be placed and by calculating how large the letters should be based on the speed of passing traffic. Get lots of pictures from many different companies to help you make your decision, and don't forget the importance of choosing the design that matches who you are as a church.

Maybe you're in the market for a new sign or you want to stick with what you have. Regardless, there are a few simple ways of increasing the effectiveness of signage. *First*, "Let there be light!" If your sign isn't lit up in some way, you've lost about 50% of your effectiveness right off the bat. While we're on the subject of outdoor lighting, some churches do shine floodlights on the front of their buildings to make them more noticeable and attractive after sundown. That's a great idea. Don't discount the extra attention a few well-placed outdoor lights can bring to your facility.

Consider another lighting option that can add some extra personality to the look of your church property. How about using landscape and accent lighting that so many people use on their homes? That leads us to tip number *two*, landscaping. Whether done by a professional or a talented group of church volunteers, great landscaping helps your building and your church sign pop right out of the ordinary scenery. Spring, summer, and fall should all find colorful flowers around your signage. Get the biggest bunch of bright flowers and the biggest bunch of eager volunteers you can find and go crazy at the base of your sign. The colorful flowers will draw the eye of passersby right to your sign where you want their attention to be. *Finally*, many church signs are designed to allow a quote or phrase to be displayed. Years ago, I saw a clever one in my hometown, "Sign broken . . . message inside." The important thing to remember here is to be committed to changing that quote on a very regular basis. If the message on your church sign hasn't been changed in a month, you're better off leaving it blank. You want to communicate freshness and attention to detail to people, not that you've been meaning to get out there and change it but just haven't had the time. What a great ministry for a volunter (as long as he can spell better than I can)! Those messages should be changed at least once a week and more often if you're in a high-traffic area. If your sign keeps changing, passersby get in the habit of looking at it. If it stays the same, they'll forget it even exists.

If your sign keeps changing, passersby get in the habit of looking at it.

Happy Holidays!

Holidays and special events are great opportunities for you to attract attention to your church building and family.

A little creativity and teamwork on outdoor displays can get the people in your town talking about your church.

We'll begin with the two most obvious times of year for outdoor church displays: Christmas and Easter. If your church doesn't do much in this category, these holidays are a great place to start. Christmas is a perfect time for us to illustrate the message of Christ to the community. Certainly it seems we are past the days of displaying the nativity on public or government property. Why don't we make an effort to remind people of the true meaning of Christmas in our own churchyards? You can spend anywhere from a few hundred dollars to several thousand building or purchasing a nativity. At the church where I grew up, we were blessed to have a very artistic man in our congregation who painted larger-than-life nativity characters onto plywood cutouts. They were beautiful. I remember looking forward to driving by the church on cold nights in December and pulling over to stare at the nativity all lit up with floodlights. It was a Christmas tradition, one that our small town came to expect every year. Your Christmas displays may be simpler or much more elaborate. Green wreaths with long red ribbons blowing in the winter wind give a pretty good look for not much money. Maybe your display consists of lots of lights or a special sign with a holiday message. An electrician in my hometown constructed a unique display for the front yard of his home. He constructed a frame and in colored Christmas lights, spelled out this message, "JUST 33 YEARS FROM THIS (a lit manger was placed there) TO THIS" (a lit cross was placed at the end of the message). Pretty effective.

Why don't we make an effort to remind people of the true meaning of Christmas in our own churchyards?

Easter is also a great chance to communicate the gospel message in a very tangible way. It could be as basic as placing three crosses on your church lawn complete with a phrase or verse of Scripture painted on a sign nearby. I can't resist telling you another story from my youth group days at

Russell Springs Christian Church. After seeing the great nativity scene our church displayed every Christmas, the youth group came up with the idea to do the same for Easter. We went to our local Christian Bookstore and purchased some detailed flannelgraph pictures that included all the characters from the crucifixion. We used an opaque projector to project the pictures onto large sheets of plywood. We traced every detail of the picture onto the board, cut the figures out, braced the cutouts and treated the wood with sealant. With some supervision and guidance, the youth group painted the figures. We reserved the faces and other difficult areas to the more talented artists in our congregation. Weeks before Easter Sunday we placed the display in the front yard. It included Christ on the cross, a Roman Soldier, a group of disciples, several women mourning, and a tomb in the background. The finished product was awesome! What a testimony to the community and we got a front-page picture and article in the local paper at no charge. There were times when traffic on Main Street would come to a near standstill as people looked at the display. On Good Friday, we took down everything but the tomb in the background and the now empty cross. Bright and early on Easter Sunday we would roll away the stone from the tomb and display the resurrected Christ figure.

Christmas and Easter aren't the only times of year you can be creative with outdoor displays. How about a sign during the Thanksgiving season that says, "Thankful for Grace," accompanied with a nice display of pumpkins, hay, and cornstalks? How about a huge flower display in springtime with a sign in the background that reads "Maybe It's Time for a Fresh Start"? Picture a heart-shaped sign on your front lawn this February that says, "God Sent You a Love Letter."

Use your imagination and creativity. The idea is to get people in the habit of looking at your facility and, in the process, they pick up little bits and pieces of information about your church and about the gospel. A minister friend told me about a lady who shook his hand after a service one Sunday. The church had just

Use your imagination and creativity.

finished their annual Easter Pageant the previous week. The lady told him that she passed the church on the way to and from work every day, but until they had put out a creative advertisement about the pageant, she never even realized there was a church there! Just because your church is located on Main Street or at a busy intersection, don't assume that everyone in town knows who you are, where you are, and what kind of church you are. It's up to you to make a great impression on the people who pass by every day. Holidays and special events can be a big help.

It's up to you to make a great impression on the people who pass by every day.

The Inside Scoop

Now let's take a look at the interior of your facility. A common misconception is that you have to bring in the wrecking ball and totally remodel to make a difference in the interior appearance of your church building. Not true. There are some simple improvements that can turn around the look of a room without calling in a construction crew. Let's discuss three hotspots that need your attention right away. Can you guess what they are?

The Foyer Comes First

Your church foyer, lobby, or "vestibule" if you're really spiritual, makes the first impression on your guests. Is your lobby area warm and welcoming or cramped and uninteresting? Think about what your mind does when you walk into someone's home or a business or a restaurant. Immediately, and many times subconsciously, you begin to develop impressions about that person or that establishment. You begin to assess the environment that you've just stepped into. The church entryway is no different for your guests and regular attendees. Your church foyer should make your guests feel welcomed and at home. It should relax them. It should demonstrate to them that you're prepared for their visit.

So how do you turn a plain lobby into a welcome mat

for guests? We'll start with the simple. If there is room in your entryway, add a sofa table up against one of the walls. This makes it feel a little bit more like home and is a great place to display information about your church (but don't overload the tabletop). While we're adding furniture items, place a lamp on the sofa table. Warm lamplight in a room can make a big difference in how welcoming it feels. A fresh coat of paint will also do wonders. Choose a warm color that coordinates with adjoining rooms. Is there room for a potted plant or two? Green plants make the room feel alive even if the plants themselves aren't. Fresh flowers every Sunday are a super nice touch, but an artificial flower arrangement is nice too, as long as it is *up-to-date*! If this country ever has a tacky, plastic flower shortage, it can quickly be resolved by raiding the flower closets of churches across the land. How about a scented candle or some nice music playing in the background? Maybe your church's foyer is approximately 4×5 and you're wondering what planet I'm on. If you have no room for furniture or plants or lamps, the very least you can do is make sure the lobby is clean, painted in an attractive color, and all the available publications are current. Along with pitching all the tacky plastic flowers, churches need to get rid of the mission newsletter updates that have been pinned to the vestibule bulletin board since 1943. Those little efforts say a lot.

The very least you can do is make sure the lobby is clean and all the available publications are current.

If you're building a facility or adding on to your existing building, I am convinced that you cannot build the lobby big enough. The lobby area has become a fellowship hall in many churches. People gather before and after services in the lobby to talk, laugh, drink coffee, and to pick up information about the church and its programs. Those are all things you want to encourage.

Are Your Restrooms Ready?

Quality restroom facilities go a long way in making a good impression on your guests. At the very least your restrooms must be clean. They must *smell* clean. That doesn't cost much at all, but if your restrooms are not clean, it may very well cost you a return visit from a guest. In today's world, updated restroom facilities are a given. Even gas stations are catching on. The church should be no exception.

If you have some money to spend on updating your restrooms, start with the ladies room. Generally speaking, women value clean, pleasant, and up-to-date facilities even more than your average guy. A few improvements can make a big difference. A full-length mirror is a nice touch and gives women a chance to take one last look before leaving the restroom. Don't forget the little details that every woman will notice. Place a basket on the sink counter with mints, facial tissue, and a few different bottles of *nice* perfume. My wife, Amanda, points out that it's important that an expensive/trendy perfume should be purchased, not the $4.95 special from the discount store. A variety of quality hairsprays are also a thoughtful addition. Amanda emphasizes the necessity of selecting *quality* products. Even if they are never used, it will make a great impression. Consider adding a colorful rug to give the feeling of home. If you have space, a small but comfortable chair is helpful to moms who have small children to take care of. If there is still room left over, add a small table with a lamp. Fresh flowers in the restroom will really surprise and impress the ladies.

There are more practical additions to be made to women's restrooms at your church. All stall doors must be functional with locks so that doors close completely. Provide small trash compartments or waste cans in *each* stall. Both the men's and women's restrooms should be equipped with wall mounted baby changing stations that are sanitized regularly. They may not be used all day, every day, but when the need arises your preparedness lets parents know you care about their needs.

Children's Areas Are No Small Matter

Visiting parents may leave their children in a less than ideal nursery or children's area once, but they will do so *only* once. Your children's areas must be a high priority. Remember that when little ones are happy and excited about church, they make sure that mom and dad know it. And I assure you that parents are looking over your children's area closely when they drop off their kids.

Following a few suggestions will make improving your children's areas as easy as ABC. *First* it's important to become a child again. Remember kids like to have fun! They love to run and jump and play and giggle. Churches, and especially children's areas in churches, should be places where kids can be kids. The Scripture reminds us that children were drawn to Jesus. I can picture Him bouncing little ones on His knee and giggling with the best of them. Make your children's areas fun and childlike. Walls, carpeting, counters, and fixtures should be bright, colorful, and fun. Many churches have used biblical themes, like Noah's Ark, Jonah and the Whale, and others to give them some direction in their decorating. That's wonderful. The key is creativity! It might even be a good idea to talk to some kids about your plans. They'll have some great ideas. In short, when guests walk into your children's rooms or down your children's hallway, they should have no doubt that they're in the children's area. If you have to use children's rooms for adult activities at other times, then let the adults put up with the kid stuff, not the other way around. Most of us adults could benefit from spending time in a fun room once in a while anyway.

I can picture Jesus bouncing little ones on His knee and giggling with the best of them.

Second, Clean children's areas are a must. Take a trip to your nursery and toddler rooms and slobber all over your hands. Then crawl around on all fours for about 10 minutes. Then suck your thumbs and other eight fingers. Don't want to? Sound disgusting? You're beginning to get an idea of how clean these areas should be. If your carpet has been there a while and you can't replace it, clean it professionally on a regular basis. Sanitize the toys every week. Keep handy wipes available for the kiddies and hand sanitizer on hand for the volunteers. Think of creative ways to display toys without cluttering up the entire space. Make sure toys are safe, without dangerous parts or tiny pieces. A clean, safe environment tells parents and your entire church that you love, respect, and value children and honor their families.

Finally, make the extra effort to be professional and caring. I know churches that change the diapers of every baby in their nursery right before mom or dad pick them up. That's extra effort. How about placing children's ministry information in a guest's diaper bag? When parents drop off their children, ask them if there are any special instructions. Remember the baby's name, and when parents return, give them a quick report of how their little one did while they were in worship. Consider using nametags and colorful aprons or smocks for your children's volunteers. It sets your volunteers apart, and parents know they're not handing over their child to just anyone.

The Eyes Have It

It really is true. A picture is worth a thousand words. Taking time to notice what's being said through your church's outdoor and indoor appearance is a big step toward becoming a people-magnet church. The challenge is to create a look, inside and out, that mirrors your church's personality. They say God is in the details. He certainly is. Use those details to your advantage. Communicate warmth and welcome to guests. Let them know you're prepared for them and you want to make their experience at your church a special one. Through intentional improvements in your church facility you can speak loudly and clearly without saying a word.

You can speak loudly and clearly without saying a word.

Chapter 5

Compelling or Selling?

Advertising and Your Church

I preached my first sermon at age 13. It was on a warm summer Sunday night at my home church in Russell Springs, Kentucky. A lot has changed in my preaching style since my inaugural sermon. I remember struggling to stretch the content so it would last twelve minutes. Now when I speak, I have to leave things out so I can stay within the time limit. I remember looking at the windows in the church to train myself to make eye contact or in that case window contact. Now I enjoy looking the audience right in the eye and trying to discern if I'm making a connection. But one thing has not changed—the importance of the message I delivered that night. The title was "Salesmen for Jesus." My dad was a traveling salesman at the time, and he and I came up with the idea together. I remember talking about how we are all Salesmen for Jesus. We must know about our "product" and how to present our product to the world. Most every Christian would agree that we should be reaching people for Jesus Christ, that Christians should be salesmen and saleswomen for Jesus. Perhaps fewer churchgoers would use those terms. There's something about sales and marketing and commercialism that makes us church folk nervous.

Oil & Water or Peanut Butter & Jelly

Do advertising and the church mix? Doesn't the straightforward nature of the gospel message stand in contrast and even repel the slick and tricky world of advertising? Doesn't the gospel demand a gimmick-free presentation? Well when you put it like that . . . yes, I think so. There's something about the message of man's sin and God's grace that doesn't fit very well with some of the advertising tactics that currently bombard our society and which, over time, our society has succumbed to and embraced. Tricking someone into becoming a follower of Christ tends to result in less than committed Christians. History has shown that converting by force doesn't produce long-lasting devotion to God. Tricks and schemes are in the same boat. But could there be room in the world of advertising for the Word of the Almighty? Maybe we could use our God-given creativity without being conniving. Maybe we could communicate the message of grace tastefully in advertising without the "infomercial" glitz.

We can use our God-given creativity without being conniving.

The answers are varied to the question, "Why don't more churches advertise and advertise effectively?" Some think advertising is much too worldly. "Church is not a business; that's a waste of God's money!" or "Word of mouth is the only appropriate way a church should advertise." These are two of the explanations we would get from those churches that choose not to advertise. I believe more often than not churches don't advertise because it simply hasn't occurred to them to try it or they tried once before and it wasn't very effective. So let's look at why churches should advertise and how they should go about it.

Why Should Churches Advertise?

Why not advertise? As you look through magazines, newspapers, watch TV, listen to the radio in your car, browse the Web, or simply look down a busy street, you'll find a million different products advertised. Each day, everything from medicine to movies, hamburgers to handbags, and cars to cat litter is advertised. Why shouldn't we advertise the most important information in human history? There is a Savior! There is hope. We have the answer not only to this life but also to eternal life: Jesus Christ. Why should we keep Him quiet? Why shouldn't we harness every means available to us to spread that good news?

Why shouldn't we advertise the most important information in human history?

In Luke 14:23 Jesus tells the story about the Great Banquet. In that story, the host of the banquet commands his servants, "Go out to the roads and country lanes and compel them to come in, so that my house will be full." In the parable the master of the banquet sends his servants out into the roads and country lanes, or as I heard it growing up, the highways and byways. Today the main roads are TV and radio. These are the means of reaching people. Today the highways are direct mail and the information superhighway. The church should not shy away from using these powerful tools. They are at our disposal to use for God's glory. Let's go out into the newspaper and the mail, the TV and the radio, and compel them to come in. I like the word, *compel*, used in this verse. That's a pretty strong word. It's more than just *make known* or *invite*. *Compel*. In other words, make a case, be convincing. Use an attractive method to show the benefit of responding. Create in the listener the desire to respond. **Compel them!** Has your church done any compelling lately? Are you compelling your community to be special guests at God's banquet table?

Galatians 4:4 says when the time had fully come, God sent His Son. I like the paraphrase, "at just the right time." I imagine God orchestrating and planning out history. God was preparing the world and all mankind for the coming of the Messiah. Thanks to the Roman Empire there was a common language and a vast road system, the combination of which made the climate just right for spreading the Word of the Savior of the world and His teachings. In other words, it was a good time to *advertise*!

When you come to think of it, God Himself might be the best advertising executive of them all. Who could resist a sky full of the Heavenly Hosts glowing bright as day and singing, "Glory to God in the highest and on earth good will to all men"? It seemed to get the attention of the shepherds, and it compelled them to travel into town and find a little baby in a trough, wrapped in rags. And what was suspended in the sky miles above that little baby? It was a star. A star that could not be overlooked. A star that inspired wonder and invited the wanderer. Don't tell me God's not into advertising.

God Himself might be the best advertising executive of them all.

Remember Jesus' first miracle, turning water to wine? When Mary suggested Jesus become the solution to the situation, He said, "My time has not yet come." In my mind I like to paraphrase that, "It's not time to advertise just yet." But we know Jesus performed a miracle that day, and with every miracle He performed, the crowds grew larger. John chapter 6 begins by telling us that large crowds were following Jesus because they had seen and heard about His healing the sick. Thousands began following Jesus because He was advertising the power and love of God. In fact, Jesus' advertising method was so effective it got Him in trouble with the religious leaders. He was becoming too popular. The people were responding too dramatically to Jesus. That response caused the religious leaders to devise a way to get rid of Him. We know that in the midst of their deceitful plan to undo Jesus, God was unfolding His beautiful plan of redemption. Even the cross itself became a billboard advertising God's grace and forgiveness and the willingness of Jesus to die in our place. There was no mistaking the message of the empty tomb. It clearly advertised—Jesus is alive!

And you can bet that any Madison Avenue ad agency would have given their collective eyeteeth to captivate audiences like Jesus did on a hillside in Jerusalem. Jaws dropped to the ground and faces were fixed on the clouds when Jesus ascended into Heaven. God advertised. He kept no secrets. Word of mouth wasn't good enough. Jesus went public. Jesus went *prime time*. God appealed to the mass audience of mankind. Our Savior shouted above the monotone rumble of everyday life and got our attention. The Creator was creative. He engaged our minds and captured our hearts when He purchased our souls!

The cross itself became a billboard advertising God's grace.

Why advertise? Because Jesus is worth it, because the gospel was lived to be told. We have more methods of spreading the message of Christ than any other people in history had. Now is the time to pour our creativity, our hearts, our minds, our passions, and our church budgets into telling that message in as many different and effective ways as humanly possible.

How Should Churches Advertise?

Most churches don't have a lot of money allocated for advertising. As your church grows and is transformed more into a people-magnet church, the advertising budget along with lots of other things may change. To begin with, however, there may not be excessive funds to work with, so *how* you advertise is very important. The truth is, creativity is more important than cash flow. You don't have to spend tens of thousands of dollars on advertising to do it well and to get results. It is necessary to be selective in choosing advertising venues and to be creative and catchy with the content and presentation of your advertising.

Often churches use their advertising dollar in a very *ordinary* way. Unfortunately these methods aren't very compelling to the unchurched. In many situations a church may be broadcasting its services on the local radio station on Sunday morning or they may occasionally put an ad in the religion section of the local paper when having a special program. Many local radio and TV stations provide community calendars or public service announcements and may read a short blurb about an upcoming church event. Most churches put their name and number in the phone book or in a listing of community churches that appears weekly in the newspaper. These may be the extent of their advertising. These advertising methods are the very tip of the possibilities iceberg.

Churches have always been a perplexing lot to me when it comes to advertising. It seems to me that some churches advertise backwards. Let me explain. Churches seem to be more apt to place an ad in the religion section of the paper, or they may use the local access channel that is dedicated to Christian programming. Many churches advertise or broadcast their ministry over the radio on Sunday morning. I've heard churches advertise outreach events and programs on Christian radio stations. *Why?* We need to ask ourselves whom we are trying to reach. If the church is trying to reach other Christians or people who go to other churches, then these methods may yield positive results. The problem is, unless we are far from hitting the mark of mission and purpose, the church exists to reach the lost. We are seeking to engage those who aren't going to church, who don't know God, who aren't connected to another church in town. Those uninvolved in the church, unfamiliar with the gospel message are our *target audience*. Put yourself in the shoes of the unbeliever for a moment. Think of yourself as the average good guy or good gal who doesn't go to church. Where are you and what are you doing on Sunday morning? I'll tell you where I'd be on Sunday morning if I weren't a Christian; I'd be asleep in bed or reading the paper over coffee, or out to breakfast with my wife. I certainly would not be listening to a sermon on the radio. Maybe I'm not the average non-Christian, but if I don't want to go to church, why would I get out of bed on Sunday at 9:30 to tune in and listen to a church service? If you were a non-Christian what sections of the paper would you read? You

We need to ask ourselves whom we are trying to reach.

might read the front page, the society page, the sports page, the funnies, but you'd probably skip right over the religion page. If I were a non-Christian and I was tooling down the highway to work, I wouldn't listen to the Christian radio station. I'd listen to the country station or the rock station or the "oldies" station, or the easy-listening station. Having said all that, why do churches spend much, if not all of their advertising dollar on Sunday mornings, on religion pages, and on Christian stations?

What's wrong with listing your events on the religion page or the Christian station? What's wrong with broadcasting your services on Sunday morning so the elderly and the sick can hear the sermon? Nothing at all. However, if you want to spend your advertising money to reach people who don't go to church or who normally wouldn't even think of your church, there are better ways. Your church must decide its mission and purpose. Once that is determined, questions like how you'll spend your advertising budget become a lot easier to answer.

A New View

Instead of thinking of advertising only as broadcasting the sermons on local radio or any free listing where you can place a blurb about a church event, develop a new view of advertising and what it could mean to your church.

In its simplest form, advertising is a vehicle, taking the viewer or listener, from one location to another. It takes people from one side and transports them to the other side. Effective advertising "morphs" people who've never tried "Burger World's" double-decker, super-duper cheeseburger into people who have. It bridges the gap between watchers, listeners, and readers and transforms them into consumers, buyers, and customers. The concept is the same when we bring advertising into the world of the church. Our goal is to bring people who don't know God into a relationship with Him. Our purpose is, by the power of God, to transform doubters, cynics, and the apathetic into seekers, believers, and faithful followers of Christ.

Compelling or Selling?

Any good businessman who has a quality product to offer and who has confidence in that product and its virtues knows all he has to do is expose the public to that product and the public will respond. The businessman would say, "I must show the public what they are missing by not using or not consuming my product." Many times I've thought that if we could only show the world what they are missing by not loving and following Christ, they would surely come around. By living the Christian life on a daily basis we show the world what they are missing. By loving one another, caring for one another, and building one another up, we show the world the virtues that are lacking from their lives. Many have not responded to Christ because they truly do not know what they are missing! Advertising is one more way we can bring that message home—literally. Advertising can go into places you will never go. It finds its way into the car, the computer, the office, and the home of the unbeliever.

Many have not responded to Christ because they truly do not know what they are missing!

When we only use the religion page of the newspaper, the Christian channel or radio station, our vehicle of advertising isn't a very effective people mover. We aren't meeting people where they are to transport them to someplace new. That's the key to great advertising. I think it's also the key to great teaching and preaching. Meet your audience where they are; it's your job to take them where you believe they need to be. This is a process. You have to do the work, not the audience. A great bridge starts where the person is and takes him to the destination. Great TV commercials, radio spots, newspaper ads, and direct mail are no different.

Creativity Makes the Difference

Remember that you don't have to spend a lot of money to see great results from advertising, but you do have to be creative. Creativity is the key to getting your money's worth. There are no discounted rates for bad or boring ads. You spend the same money whether your commercial has pizzazz or barely has a pulse, so it's to your advantage to put a lot of thought into your advertising. What a great opportunity to get people in your church involved! We're always asking for volunteers for the nursery, to visit people in the hospital or to sing a solo. I bet there are people in your congregation who may not have gifts in those areas but who are very talented when it comes to bringing a concept to life using art, humor, computer design, or written copy. In the process of putting together a great ad, you may discover a group of very gifted people who, until they joined the advertising team, had felt left out of the picture. (Don Waddell's book, *Making Your Church a Place to Serve: Involving Members the Southeast Way*, suggests ways members can discover their God-given talents.)

There are no discounted rates for bad or boring ads.

Once you've gathered your advertising gurus together how should you get started? One guiding principle for you to consider is to make the time together fun. Meetings that are structured, cold, and follow a rigid schedule have never been famous for churning out creative ideas. Consider beginning your meeting by watching TV or a homemade videotape of TV commercials. Discuss why each ad appeals or doesn't appeal to you. What are some of your favorite ads on TV, and why do you like them? What makes a good commercial? The answers to these questions can be applied to your ad whether you're planning to use TV, radio, the paper, direct mail, or other methods to get your message out into the community. Maybe your group's favorite ads are funny, feature cute kids as the star, or communicate an unexpected message that doesn't become clear until the last seconds of the ad. As a team, talk about how you can use some of the same frameworks to make the contents of your advertisement come to life.

Keep in mind that no idea is a bad idea while you're in the brainstorming phase of creating. Throw out questions, and then record every idea with colored markers on a posterboard, newsprint flip chart, or whiteboard so everyone can see your progress. Ask, "In one catchy phrase, how would you describe our church to the community?" "How would you describe what people are missing by not being part of a church family?" "What do you think is the funniest misconception people have about church and church people?" By asking questions like this you may stumble across a sentence that could carry an entire advertising campaign. Picture it on direct mail pieces, on billboards in town, on the radio, in the paper, and on TV. WOW! Dream about how your community would begin to notice your church! Imagine how some of those people would begin to get curious enough to try attending your church one weekend or during a special event designed for them simply because of the theme of your advertising blitz.

Spend several energetic meetings on developing the concept and direction of your advertising. Don't shortchange this step in the process. The more prayer, thought, and creativity you pour into this phase of the adventure, the more effective your end product, and the better use of your budgeted money. Hey, by the time you involve several people in this ministry, you may have generated special offerings for the ads as well as excitement!

Next, try assigning different people on the team to investigate the various forms of advertising. Give one person TV commercials, another newspaper ads, another radio, and so on. You could also ask representatives from the sales departments of these companies to visit your meeting and share the benefits of using their medium to communicate to your city. It may be a good idea to let them know where you are in the process, that no sales will take place at the informational meeting, and determine a specific time limit. Most companies would be happy to send someone over to talk with your team.

Some Beginning Tips

You'll find some resources listed in the back of this book. In the meantime, here are a few tips and idea appetizers to get you ready to dig in!

Become Front-Page News

Try "theming" your ads to the sections of the newspaper. For example, maybe you are advertising a sermon series on how to make your marriage work. Why not place those cleverly worded ads on the Society page where wedding announcements are found? The sports section of your local paper during baseball season sure would be just the ticket for an ad that read "Three strikes and you're out! Rules of the game or rules for life? Ever wonder what God thinks when we strike out?" Design your ad to look like a story in the paper, complete with an outrageously funny headline about church.

Try "theming" your ads to the sections of the newspaper.

Get People Tuned In

If radio ads sound like the right frequency for your church, consider placing ads on the popular stations at drive times, the times during the day when most people are driving to and from work (7:00–9:00 am and 5:00–6:00 pm). These time slots give you a chance at catching the ear of a great many people in your area. Thirty-second spots (or commercials) at these times may be very effective for your church. Take a listen to the local rock, country, or "oldies" station at these times. You could be the only church advertising on the station during these time slots. That's great! Your ad will really make a statement to the listeners. While we're on the subject, consider what kind of statement you want to make to the listeners. After hearing your ad on the radio, would they get the impression that your church is contemporary or traditional, family focused, or designed with Gen-Xers in mind? Maybe your ads will communicate short teachings from Scripture that are very applicable to everyday life, communicating that your goal is to make the Scripture relative to their situation. Follow it up with "brought to you by so and so church." Whether you're "driving home" a serious message, taking your listener by surprise with humor, or just trying to describe your church in a creative way, be purposeful in the planning of your airtime and you'll perk some ears.

Be purposeful in the planning of your airtime.

Special Delivery

Direct Mail is one way to get the word out in your community. There are companies, those that specifically serve churches and those that don't, that do a great job at making their mailing pieces look like anything but junk mail. It has always amazed me how much a little 8″ × 5″ postcard can say about your church. Check out some of my favorite companies listed in the suggested resources on page 125 and request their free information and samples. You'll be pleasantly surprised! I have also designed a direct mail piece myself for a church where I served. I know many churches that have put together their own piece. Don't be afraid to give it a try if you believe you have something unique to say to your community. You may want to consider a series of mailers that all relate to one another and that would be sent out over a period of a month or so. That repeated appearance in the stack of mail on the kitchen table may appeal to the best of someone's curious side.

TV?! Are You Crazy?

Maybe you're thinking, "TV commercials are a kazillion bucks a minute! My church doesn't have that kind of money!" Now that you've gotten that off your chest, consider a surprising fact: your local cable company can place your commercial not just on the local-access channel, but on the major network channels as well. It's also much more affordable than you might imagine. When you consider the impact a quality commercial could have on your ministry, it's worth looking into. There are local companies that will produce great commercials for you, but there are also national companies with a group of wonderful commercials already produced that you can choose from. The company adds your church's name at the end of the spot and that's it!

Again, viewing the free video and information available from church commercial companies will get any church group interested in the possibility of reaching your area with a powerful message.

Sow Some Advertising Seed

In the Parable of the Sower (Matthew 13) Jesus talks about the different types of ground on which the seed falls. Some ground was hard, some rocky, some thorny, and some soft and fertile. The sower is never guaranteed that all the seed will take root, grow, and yield fruit. But never in that parable does the sower consider keeping the seed to himself. There are certainly no guarantees when we advertise what our churches and ultimately what Christ Himself has to offer, but that is no reason why the limitless possibilities of today's advertising world should go unused for God's glory. Spread the word! Go therefore. Send the light. Compel them!

If God can use a burning bush or a child's lunch or, most amazing of all, people like you and me to reach others with His power and love, then I am sure He can use an ad or a commercial or a postcard. Maybe one day some of the most active people in your church will be the folks who read your ad on the sports page and wondered what kind of church would put an ad on the sports page. Or it could be the teenager who heard the radio spot that didn't bother using big religious words and spoke directly to his life while he was listening to the rock station in his car. Maybe it will be the single mom who flipped through junk mail one day and discovered a church that cared about the future of her and her children. Take the chance and see what God might do when we communicate His love in a relevant, applicable, compelling way.

Chapter 6

Getting Personal

A Visitor Just Showed Up . . . Now What?

Let's just say for the sake of this chapter that your church has done a fantastic job at everything we've discussed so far. You've defined your mission as a church and chosen the methods by which you are going to communicate the message. You've discerned the perception people in your community have of your church and you've discovered a perception that more accurately depicts the type of church you are. You've even made some amazing and head-turning strides in the realm of indoor and outdoor appearances. The team has ripped out everything from the old sign to the shag carpet and everything but the preacher has had a new paint job and a facelift. Advertising? You better believe it! People all over town are commenting about the hysterical mailings they're getting from your church, and people listening to your radio ads in their cars are nearly causing accidents they love them so much. Things are going

When God blesses your church with visitors, what do you do with them?

great! You and the teams of involved volunteers have bathed every step of this process in prayer, and God is blessing in great ways. In fact, it's Sunday morning, and there are three visitors who are checking out the church as we speak! One problem. What do we do with these visitor-people now that they're showing up?

We all know that in the real world it takes more than reading about it to make it happen. If it were that simple, just reading the Scripture would—*poof*—turn us into perfect followers of Christ and we wouldn't even need to be talking about any of this. Everything suggested in this resource takes time and is subject to failure. God guides each of us and the churches we serve as He chooses. He may have different plans altogether. He decides how He will bless and lead; we wouldn't want it any other way. But when God does bless your church with visitors, as He may already do every single weekend, what do you do with them? Are you prepared for them? What do they experience? How do they feel after they've spent five minutes in your midst, and how do they feel five minutes after they've left the parking lot?

Aren't You a Hotel?

Allow your mind to use your imagination as a sketchpad for a minute. Imagine a lavish hotel. Picture the detailed swirls in the marble steps as you approach the entrance. Notice the potted palms gently swaying in the evening breeze. Let the glow of the rich lighting inside catch your eye. Now, step through the threshold giving a thankful nod to the gentleman in uniform and white gloves who opened the door for you and greeted you by name. The lobby is magnificent isn't it? Straight ahead you notice beautiful marble columns dancing around a spiral staircase. To your right, plush furniture tries to coax you over, inviting you to relax and unwind. You proceed to your right where the mahogany front desk awaits your effortless check-in. You are shown to your room. "If the hallway looks this amazing," you wonder to yourself, "my suite must be unbelievable!" The bellhop throws open the double doors to your suite. The doors open in slow motion, and you hear the brush of harp strings. Still holding your breath, you gaze into your room. *The needle screeches across the record!* "***What!*** How could this be?" you shout in disappointment. "Something is very wrong with this picture!" Your room is empty. There is nothing. No bed. No furniture. No shower. No carpet. No drapes. No pillow. No potted palm. Nothing. Nothing but concrete walls and a concrete floor. I don't know what you do next, but in my little dream world I march right down to the mahogany front desk and I ring the little brass bell. "Excuse me," I say, "I have a problem. My suite is empty. There's no bed, no shower, no TV, no robe with the hotel's initials on it, no potted palm, ***nothing***! You are a hotel, aren't you? All this stuff in the lobby is nice, but when you boil it all down, I came here to relax, sleep, and shower!"

The point is, there are some necessities that a hotel must provide its guests if it's to be considered a hotel. The hotel must provide a place to sleep and a place for its guests to get ready the next morning. Without that, you can't really say it's much of a hotel. The church is no different. We can have a nice lobby and great parking. We can spruce up the exterior of the building and advertise. We can display our mission statement in letters of fire, 10-feet tall, but if we do not provide a connection to God's Word and our Savior, Jesus Christ, through people who live by the Word and who know and love that Savior, we can't really be called a church. Once the visitor is prompted to show up on your doorstep, your ministry has only just begun. Everything leading up to and contributing to that initial visit is only a very small part of the equation. People are looking for God. They are looking for hope. They are looking for a way out or a way up. They are looking for an answer. They are looking for a roadmap to negotiate life. They are looking for love, significance, belonging—a home. If you have all the bells and whistles

If we do not provide a connection to God, we aren't really a church.

like great parking and funny ads and nice buildings but you don't deliver when it comes to the *real* reason they came, they might ask, "You are a church, aren't you?"

The personal touch cannot be underestimated. The importance of a church full of loved and forgiven people ready to love and forgive others cannot be glossed over. The power of personal connection is priceless to anyone who walks through the doors of your church, because it is in the initial moments of connecting with someone personally that they begin to make a connection with God. We are Christ's ambassadors, His hands, His smile, His heart. Let's talk about some of the finer points of getting personal with your church's guests.

The Great Wall of Preconceptions

In most situations in which you and I find ourselves, we subconsciously develop preconceptions about what we are about to experience. How many times have you thought, "This isn't what I expected," as you critiqued an experience? Accurate or not, you often make a judgment based on your assumptions of how circumstances would unfold.

Don't you imagine the guests that visit your church for the first time arrive with some preconceptions? Maybe some of them are good, but if the person is a bit skeptical of church or maybe if he hasn't been to church in several years, odds are good that there are some pretty scary assumptions floating around in his mind. I call it *The Great Wall of Preconceptions* because it is a barrier that is built between that person and the actual experience. Picture each brick in the wall labeled with a different preconception. A guest may have preconceptions like some of these:

First-time guests to your church arrive with their own preconceptions.

"I'm not going to meet anyone who really wants to get to know me."

"My life is too full of mistakes to even be seen in a church."

"I'll bet my clothes aren't good enough to wear here."
"These people have all the answers."
"This church is too big—I'll never get to know anybody."
"This church is too small—everybody will stare at me."

One by one these preconceptions get stacked up, and by the time the person walks into your services there's a distance there, a wall of separation. It ought to be our goal to tear down that wall brick by brick. The Great Wall of Preconceptions should crumble a little bit more each time a guest encounters someone from your church. Whether the church-goer is a Greeter or a Welcome Center Volunteer or simply a regular attendee, everyone can participate in tearing down the wall and removing those barriers. Every effort you make to help your guest feel welcome and at home, every smile, every "Good morning, my name is . . ." removes a brick.

The Smile and the Extra Mile

Tearing down The Great Wall of Preconceptions does not take a degree in structural engineering. It is not rocket science! Start with this principle, the smile and the extra mile. See, it's simple. The *first* component is . . . *Smile*! Smiling doesn't cost the people of your church or your church budget a single cent. It's free, but it is worth so very much. By simply smiling you can turn up the energy in a room in a matter of seconds. When you begin to discuss this with your congregation or with a team of volunteers, ask them to help you conduct an important experiment. Tell the group, on the count of three, you want them to smile the biggest smiles possible on their faces and turn to the people seated around them and show off their smile. 1-2-3. Watch the room instantly and drastically change its personality! If you can remind the people of your church to notify their faces that they are saved and going to heaven, it will really make a difference.

Remind the people of your church to notify their faces that they are saved.

Not only will smiling make a difference to your guests who experience a positive atmosphere, it will also help those who are there every week look forward to being in a place of joy. I'm not talking about being fake. Church should be a place where we can be authentic with one another, even in times of struggle or heartache. But on the whole, we have a great deal to smile about. If the church where you attend and serve isn't a happy place where laughter and smiles come pretty naturally, make it your personal mission to transform it into such a place! Imagine yourself as an apprehensive first-time visitor. You walk in and scan a sea of sour, sad, or just plain bored faces. Now imagine backing up and getting back in your car! Who wants to be in a place where rain clouds follow everyone around? People are attracted to happy, joyful, positive people. How many times have you heard people say, "Hey, let's go talk to Joe. He's always negative and never cracks a smile!"? It just doesn't happen. When it comes to the personal touch, don't underestimate the effect a positive, smiling congregation can have on a hesitant guest. You make approximately eleven different impressions about a person in the first seven to ten seconds of meeting her. Smiling goes a long way in making a good first impression.

Don't underestimate the effect a positive, smiling congregation can have on a hesitant guest.

The *second* half of this no-brainer formula is *The Extra Mile*! Constantly instill in the people of your church the importance of having an extra-mile attitude. It's important for everyone in your church to exhibit this attitude, but it's absolutely essential for those who serve in your hospitality ministry. This attitude of service and flexibility will make any ministry endeavor run much smoother. There is certainly no substitute for an extra-mile, servant's-heart attitude when it comes to serving your guests.

Shortly after my wife and I moved into our first home together, a two-bedroom apartment, I made a trip to a nationally known hardware store. To fully appreciate this story, you have to know that I'm about as adept at fixing things as I am at performing brain surgery. I walked into the hardware store and with the deer-in-the-headlights look in my eyes, feverishly searched for someone to help me. I needed a part for hooking up my clothes-dryer, you know, a thingamajig. Finally, I found a salesperson and asked for the part. "It's over there," he said, as he motioned to the back of the warehouse. "Go down this aisle, make a left, go two more aisles down and hang a right, you find the part you need about a quarter of the way down the aisle on the bottom shelf." While I'm sure the directions made sense to him, I didn't have much luck finding the much-needed thingamajig. As I spent 10 minutes scouring the shelves for the part, I thought, "Thank you ***so much*** for your time, Mr. Home Improvement Center; you really do have a way of serving customers! Sorry to interrupt you on your way to the soda machine." I left and went down the road to another nationally known hardware center where I asked for the same thingamajig. You'll never guess what happened. The gentleman smiled and said, "Sure, I know where that is, follow me." As we approached the part he picked it off the rack and handed it to me. "Do you have everything else you need for the job, sir?" He politely asked. I did have everything else I needed, but I wanted to buy more stuff anyway! Who knew purchasing a thingamajig could be such a pleasant experience? Do I need to tell you where I do all my hardware shopping now? I think you know.

That's the basic idea behind an extra-mile attitude. Now think about the many times a guest has asked someone in your church where the nursery or the bathroom or the such-and-such class meets. Do people in your church or in your hospitality ministry say, "Back that way," gesturing in midair as they rattle off meaningless directions? I hope not. I hope they say, "Sure, I know where that is, follow me. By the way, my name is Mark. Have you been coming to First Church for a while?" Suddenly, more than a trip to the such-and-such class occurs. Maybe a friendship begins.

In Matthew 5:41, during Jesus' Sermon on the Mount, He astounds His listeners by saying, "If someone forces you to go one mile, go with him two miles." In other words, go the extra mile. Jesus is speaking to Jews who are in a Roman-occupied territory. By law, if a Roman soldier was passing through town, he could command any Jew to walk with him and carry his luggage. What a pain in the neck! Can you imagine being in the middle of gardening or feeding your animals or washing your clothes and having some smelly soldier make you stop what you're doing to carry his bags? The law specified, however, that the Jew only had to walk one mile with the Roman. Along the roads leading out of little villages the people would drive a stake into the ground as a mile marker. I picture the people reaching the mile marker, not taking one step past the stake and dropping the bags in the dust. Think about the impact it would have on a Roman soldier when a follower of Christ passed the mile marker. What if the follower of Christ spent those two or three miles talking with the soldier, asking about his family and his work, showing genuine concern and care, all the while lugging the heavy baggage? WOW! That makes a statement, doesn't it? That's just what Jesus had in mind. Maybe we should not only greet people at the front doors of our churches, but also start helping with diaper bags. Maybe we should hang up a few coats and show guests to their destination, not just give them directions.

Maybe we should not only greet people at the front doors of our churches, but also start helping with diaper bags.

One Sunday morning, at the church where I serve, a greeter named Samantha Johnston noticed a lady walking through the front door covered in children and diaper bags. Sam, as she is called, discerned this was the guest's first visit to our church from the look of confusion on her face. Sam approached her, gave a warm "good morning" and asked, "Would you like me to help you get your children checked into our Children's Ministry?"

"That would be wonderful!" the guest bubbled in relief. Sam grabbed a few diaper bags and the group headed for the Children's Ministry. As Sam introduced herself and got to know the guest a little, she learned that this indeed was her first visit. She was in a neighborhood Bible study with a woman from our church, and she finally decided to give church a try. The three children were all different ages and therefore in different areas of our children's department. After the children were all checked into their different areas, the guest told Sam, "This church is so big," and then half-kidding, half serious she said, "I'll never find my kids again."

"No problem," Sam reassured, "my husband is saving me a seat in the sanctuary. Why don't you sit with me during the service, and when it's over, I'll come back with you and we'll pick up your kids." WOW! That's extra-mile service!

The church should be a place where sincere relationships can be started on visit number one.

The extra-mile attitude can make all the difference and convey the personal touch that people miss out on so many times. The church should be a place where sincere relationships can be started on visit number one. Getting personal with a smile and the extra mile helps in making that a reality.

Don't Be Afraid

Often people are afraid to make the first move and approach those at church they don't know. "What if I ask them if it's their first Sunday and they get insulted because they've been coming to church here for 50 years?" church members often ask me. I say, "So what!" Seriously, why let something like that keep you from welcoming a guest or from meeting someone for the first time? Introduce yourself. Ask their names. Ask how long they've been coming. If they say, "This is my first week"—BINGO! God just made an appointment for you to meet a new friend to encourage and love. If they say they've been going to this church for the last 26 years, 10 months and 2 weekends, laugh and say something like, "Isn't it funny that we've never really talked?" Then get to know your fellow charter member!

Everyone's personality is different. For some, talking to a stranger comes naturally. For others, doing such a thing is unthinkable. If you're in the latter category, why not ask God to give you some extra courage and take a flying leap right out of your comfort zone this Sunday. Who knows what God will do? You won't unless you give it a try. There are visitors among you who don't want to be visitors for long. They may not act like it at first, but they need the personal touch of a smile, a caring word, and a new friend who is sincerely interested in who they are. After all, *you are a church, aren't you?*

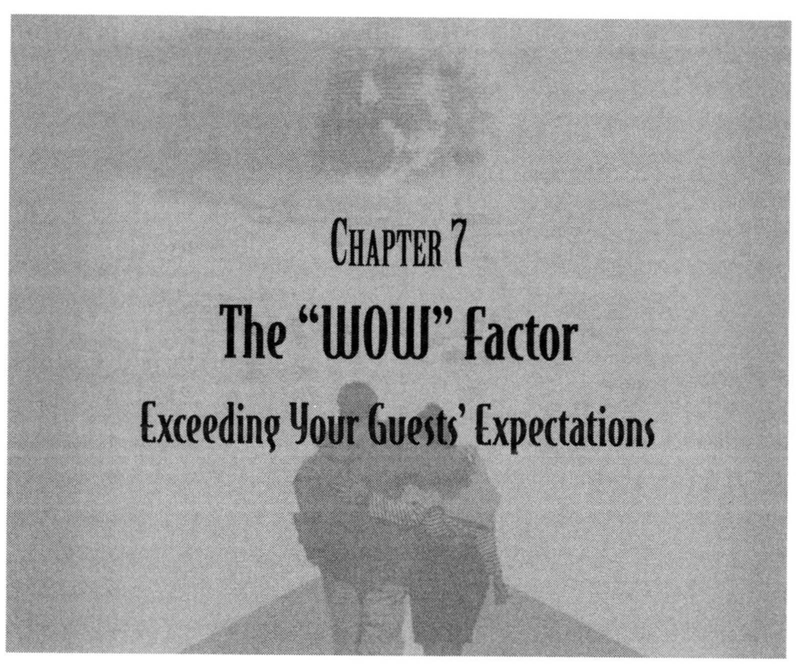

Chapter 7

The "WOW" Factor

Exceeding Your Guests' Expectations

See if you can identify with this common experience. The other day I pulled into the drive-through of a fast food restaurant. I waited at the menu board for someone to take my order. Finally I am greeted with a "Can I take your order?" I proceed to order my lunch and the person on the other end repeats not my order, but perhaps the guy's order 3 cars ahead of me. Maybe the little headphones the person wears picked up another transmission from a fast food place across town, who knows? We all finally agree on what I ordered and I pull around to the pick-up window. Suddenly a hand emerges from the restaurant, "$4.37" comes from inside the building. I hand over my money. Then, the same hand emerges again, this time holding a bag. That's it. Nothing else. No words, no sounds, nothing. I say, "Thank you," because I can hardly stand the rude silence. I drive off and enjoy a lovely meal.

The checkout line at the grocery store is no different. Each time I am there I get the same treatment from the teenagers at the checkout. They barely make eye contact with the customer, and do not greet a single person in line. I guess they are too busy flirting with the other teenage employees. Many times the checkout clerk will carry on a conversation with someone nearby the entire time she is ringing up my purchase, never once acknowledging my presence. Very seldom is even a halfhearted "thank you" muttered.

I am continually surprised how many poor or, at best, mediocre, customer service situations people experience today. Sometimes you would think you've ruined someone's day by being her customer. Occasionally I feel as though I've burdened the person behind the counter by handing him my money. Sure, I realize it's just a cheeseburger, it's just a pack of gum or a few gallons of gas, but does it really take that much effort to say, "Thank you. Have a nice day"? On the bright side, you learn to really appreciate it when someone smiles at you and says, "Thank you, sir, have a great day and come back again."

Once in a while I am "WOWED" by the customer service I receive.

Once in a while, however, I am "WOWED" by the customer service I receive. Some time ago my wife Amanda and I went into a local pizza place. Some teenagers greeted us from behind the counter. They were some of the nicest teenagers I had talked to in a long time. It was also a great pizza buffet. The teens told us what was on the buffet, showed us where everything was and also offered to make us a fresh pizza if we wanted something different besides what was out on the buffet. They were very pleasant, conversational, and sincere. It was an excellent experience. We shared that with the manager on the way out. When we left that day I said, "Wow, I've never been treated so nice in a pizza place before."

My wife told me about a great customer service moment she witnessed in our local drugstore. She was in line to get some film developed when she noticed an employee leaving from the back room. It was obvious that he was off the clock and on his way out the door. He had taken off his nametag and anything else that would distinguish him as an employee. Seconds later an elderly man asked if the store carried a specific item. He paused for a moment and then responded, "We sure do, follow me. I'll show you right where it is." Right after that someone else approached him in search of another product. He took him to the item he was looking for. WOW! He could have ignored the customers altogether or simply mumbled, "Aisle six," as if his entire day had just been ruined. Or, he could have even kindly passed those folks off to another employee, but he didn't. That's great customer service!

A Tale of Two Experiences

How does your church stack up? After guests pay you a visit, what do they say to one another on the way to the car? Let's start with the desired end result and work our way backward. The goal is for guests to leave your church thinking and saying, "WOW!" Think of the impact your church would have on the guest. Don't forget the countless people the guest will tell about his or her WOW experience. That's right, there are more than just immediate benefits to wowing your Sunday morning visitors. Guests can either be ambassadors or ambushers of your church. If their experience is mediocre (just what they expected) or if their experience is poor, not only do you lose that guest probably forever, but you lose their friends and family and the guy in the cubical across from him at work.

Guests can either be ambassadors or ambushers of your church.

"I tried Community Church Sunday." The conversation might begin, "It reminded me why I haven't been to church in 13 years. I walked in and out of that place, and the only person who said a word to me was the preacher, and that's what he gets paid to do. This one lady looked at me like I had three heads, I guess 'cause I wasn't wearing a suit. I don't fit in there at all and I'm not going back to be treated like an outcast!"

Ouch! Wouldn't you love to hear some of the after-church comments from your visitors? I hope none of them leave feeling like this guy. On the other hand, what if the gentleman in question had gone to Community Church and had a WOW experience? Maybe his conversation on Monday morning would have been dramatically different.

"You'll never guess what I did yesterday. I went to church. I know it's been years since I went to church, but I really liked it. I went to Community Church just off of highway 51. I walked up to the front door, and this guy opened the door for me and welcomed me. He started a conversation with me right there on the front porch. Then before I could get through the lobby, two other people said good morning, and a young couple, John and Jennifer, introduced themselves to me. They ended up sitting with me. After the service John gave me his e-mail address and told me if I had any questions to drop him a line. Turns out we work out at the same gym and we're going to meet Thursday morning. On my way out someone gave me a basket of cookies and some information about the church. Everyone was so easy to talk to! I have never been treated so well at church in my entire life!" Now that's a WOW experience! Don't you think that's the way church *should be*?

I think it's a real shame when I pay four bucks for a value meal and get it handed to me without a thank you or without a single word at all. But that cannot compare to the tragedy of someone giving church a try for the first time in a long time or the first time in his life and then walking out the door never to return because you and I dropped the ball. We were too wrapped up in our own little world to make a difference in the world of the guest. That was God's guest walking out the door. The fact is we have a responsibility to make our church guest's experience a WOW experience. Most of the time your church has only one shot at making an impression on a visitor. Have there been times when your church has blown it?

We have a responsibility to make our church guest's experience a WOW experience.

Have visitors left your church never to return because it wasn't a WOW experience? Don't dwell on the missed opportunities; focus on the future and what can be accomplished for God. Your church can WOW the guests that God will send your way.

The Way to "WOW"

I don't think wowing the average church visitor is all that difficult. I do think too few churches give the idea that much consideration. There are some simple steps you can take to make a big difference and to get your church well on its way to becoming a wowing church. Before we look at those steps, take a look at this story from Ron Willingham's book, *Hey, I'm The Customer*:

> Visiting a dental office isn't at the top of most people's list of memorable experiences, is it? But then, most people have never been to see Dr. Ron Bentham of Country Pines Dental Centre in Penticton, British Columbia. Ron Bentham's dental office is, well, not exactly like most other dental offices you've visited. For starters, it looks like a comfortable home as you drive up to it. Upon entering, you walk into, not a typical waiting/reception room, but a giant country kitchen complete with a harvest table, chairs, and colonial William Bradford upholstered chairs. The beautiful colors and tasteful appointments make a very pleasing visual appearance, but the most impressive sensory impression is yet to come. Patients are greeted with, not the typical smells of a dental office, but with the pleasant aroma of freshly baked muffins. Yeah, muffins! Upon entering, each person is offered one of these wonderfully smelling delicacies. The menu changes daily—blueberry one day, applesauce the next, and so on. Patients are also offered them when they leave the office. Needless to say, they leave with a lasting impression of their visit to the dental office. But that's not all. Dr. Bentham also has fresh-cut flowers in the reception room each day. Most of the

> people receive a flower when they leave. He offers a pick-up service for senior citizens. On their way home his driver will even stop by the supermarket or other places where his patients need to stop.

Now that's a WOW experience. Wouldn't you agree? Dr. Bentham has made a WOW experience out of something that people hate, dread, and avoid! We need that kind of passion for WOW experiences in our churches!

There are six different steps to wowing your guests. I see them at work in this story of The Patient-driven Dentist. The six steps or principles of WOW are as follows: 1. Be prepared for the guest. 2. Make an impression immediately. 3. Offer a unique approach. 4. Go above and beyond what is expected. 5. Give the guest a gift. 6. Make the experience memorable. Let's take a look at each of those in detail.

1. Be prepared for the guest.

Take a clue from the Boy Scouts—be prepared! Developing an attitude of preparation for your guests is half the battle. Expect them. Pray for them. Prepare for them. There is nothing worse than having a party guest show up 20 minutes early when you're just not ready yet. Just when you think you have all the time in the world to complete the final preparations, you hear the paralyzing ring of the doorbell. Your security is dissolved and panic sets in. Don't let that happen at church! Be prepared for your guests. "Yeah," you might say, "but we haven't had a visitor at our church for about a year and a half." That's my point exactly! Why would God send visitors in your direction if your church weren't ready for them?

Developing an attitude of preparation for your guests is half the battle.

There's a difference in how you see your house if you are home for a lazy Sunday afternoon as opposed to the way you see your house if you are expecting six people for dinner. When you're expecting guests, you see your surroundings with a more critical eye. Give your church facility, your programs, and your worship service that critical eye! Put out the welcome mat so to speak.

Do you have any doubt about Dr. Bentham being prepared for his patients? No doubt, whatsoever. Everything he did showed that the patients, his customers, were on his mind. He was prepared for their arrival, for their visit, and for their departure. Everything from the first impression to the driver who took elderly patients home or by the supermarket illustrates the fact the Dr. B is prepared. WOW. Are you prepared for guests at your church? Do you and those who make up your Guest Services or Hospitality Ministry bustle around the church before services making sure the details are covered, that everything's in place, that every door has a smiling, outgoing greeter nearby? Being prepared says so much to your guests. It lets them know that you are expecting them. You have planned ahead of time to ensure their experience is a great one.

2. Make an impression immediately.

You can make an impression with no effort at all, but the impression you give might be, "We don't want you here." "You're intruding on our little club; hit the road!" If your desire is to make a good impression, focus on making that positive impression as soon as possible. In Dr. Bentham's case, we see that immediately his patients were impressed because the building they drove up to didn't look like a dentist's office at all. Instead of the cold, institutional look of an office building or some medical buildings, they are impressed immediately with the neighborhood atmosphere of the house converted into an office. Not only that, but right away, from the first second they step foot in the front door, they are carried across the threshold by the sweet smells of fresh, hot muffins. Stepping into the kitchen, the heart of the home, isn't a bad touch either. Right away the patients are put at ease by their surroundings, and all their senses are involved. What changes could you make at your church so that all of

Focus on making your positive impression as soon as possible.

your guests' senses are immediately and pleasantly involved? What would it take to put them at ease right away? Making a good impression from the get-go is invaluable. Take an inventory of *firsts*. What are the first things your visitors see? What are the first things your visitors smell and hear and touch and taste? Who are the first people your visitors come in contact with?

If you are missing opportunities to make a great impression on your guests in the first few seconds and minutes of their time with you, put a stop to those wasted moments. Try some new things that *will* make a difference. Place the right people at the front door or on the porch. Spruce up the looks of your lobby area, making it feel a little warmer and a bit more like home. Is it possible to place a coffee pot off to the side with some muffins, donuts, or cookies? Just think, even if no one took a single cookie or a single cup of coffee (yeah, right), the smell of the percolating coffee would fill the air and the stacks of baked goodies would say to those who pass by, "You're welcome here, and we want you to have a wonderful morning."

3. Offer a unique approach.

In this category we have a great advantage. Our advantage is, people expect a church to look and feel a certain way when they walk in. That means that with a little creativity we can make a great impact on people. Uniqueness is really lacking in churches today. For some reason we got fooled into thinking there's only one way to "do church." Nonsense! There are as many different ways of doing the church *thing* as there are churches! I don't mean doctrine or message; I mean method.

People are flabbergasted with wonder and excitement when they go to Dr. Bentham's place because they've never been in a dentist office that was anything like that their entire life! Every dentist office they've ever been in has been the same boring place. But now that they've found a unique approach to dentistry, they'll never be happy anywhere else. When your guests step through the door of your church, they expect the same boring church deal that they've seen or heard about all their lives. Why don't you think of some ways to surprise their seekin' socks off? Show them that you have a unique approach to church, and they'll never be happy anywhere else.

Show them that you have a unique approach to church, and they'll never be happy anywhere else.

It's a good thing I'm not a church architect because I'd probably get laughed out of every meeting. I'd propose church lobbies that were about half as big as the sanctuary instead of the little cracker box lobbies we're used to. I would design an enormous open kitchen on one end of the lobby with a huge 30-foot serving bar (not that kind of bar; you know, a serving bar like the kind in your kitchen at home). I'd install skylights and I'd use lots of stone and beautiful woods and materials that make you feel like you just stepped into a bed and breakfast. I would make the church sign a contract stating that the sweetest women in the whole church (and a few nice men) would be in that kitchen every Sunday serving up the best coffee, and baked goods so tasty and fresh they'd make even the vilest pagan burst into the "Hallelujah Chorus." Those friendly folks in the kitchen would know the answers to the questions you'd normally get asked at the Welcome Center. Beside the open kitchen I'd design a sunken living room area with lots of big sofas and chairs and church information on the coffee tables. And don't forget the big stone fireplace! Tell me that wouldn't get some visitors talking on Monday morning at work. Tell me that wouldn't make people relax and feel at home right away. Tell me that wouldn't communicate, "We love you; we're prepared for you; we want your experience here to be special." Tell me why we're so afraid to be creative and unique.

4. Go above and beyond what is expected.

Ask yourself what a guest might expect at a church. Then go above and beyond that expectation. Would guests expect someone to kindly tell them where the nursery is? Then walk them to the nursery! While you're walking, ask them about their children and tell them about the Children's Ministry of your church. When you arrive at the nursery, introduce the baby and parent both by name to the nursery volunteer. Would a guest expect to be invited back? Send them an engraved invitation to return in the mail. Follow it up with a phone call or a basket of homemade cookies on their doorstep. After asking a Welcome Center Volunteer about the single adult Sunday school class, a guest might expect to hear the name of the class and when and where the class meets. Why not also give the guest a flyer outlining all the classes you offer and a listing of single adult activities and events? Let him know you'd be happy to add him to the single adult mailing list. Before leaving church, give the guest's name to one of the single adult ministry leaders who would give him a call to answer any questions and encourage him to show up to the next scheduled event.

Going above and beyond is really a fun challenge.

Going above and beyond is really a fun challenge. It's fun to see what you can do to take serving someone to the next level. Challenge the volunteers in your Hospitality Ministry to discover the joy of "above and beyond" service. Provide a special card where they can record how they went above and beyond in a situation. That way you stay informed on the neat ways people are being served in the church. It also gives leaders a chance to tell another volunteer what a great job they're doing, not to mention it provides you with lots of good examples of above and beyond service to share with other volunteers and leaders.

5. Give the guest a gift.

What you offer the guests as a gift is less important than the fact that you've made an effort to show your appreciation for their visit. Gifts like a coffee mug with your church's name printed around the sides is a great gift. Filling the mug with information, candy, or other treats makes a great impression. Consider a small basket with candy or cookies with some church information tucked away in the back. The secret once again is creativity. Are there everyday objects that you can use in a unique way to make a great gift? You can have your church's name printed on everything from Frisbees to a can of mixed nuts. Maybe your welcome team will select something the guest might use on a regular basis to print your church name or logo on. I've heard stories of West Coast churches whose gifts match the culture their church is surrounded by. They give away beach towels to their guests. The church logo and information are printed nicely on the towels. Another gives out supersippers with the church information inside. Sermon tapes also make great gifts. On the reverse side, include a welcome from the minister or testimonials from church members about what the church has meant to them and how they got more involved. Consider a gift certificate to a local restaurant or ice cream shop. There may be restaurant owners or business people in your church who would be delighted to give the church a discounted rate on a large number of gift certificates. If you're really serious about making a connection with your guests on their first visit, and your budget will allow it, select a friendly couple from the congregation who are involved and know a great deal about the church and have them take visitors to lunch compliments of the church. Talk about a WOW experience. Even if the guests don't take you up on the first invitation, they might come back the next week and be ready to interact and ask questions over lunch, or they may decline but be impressed by your sincere invitation. What a great opportunity not only to make them feel welcomed and develop relationships, but to ask about their experience and observations. Your guest lunch couple may come back from the meal with two or three new ideas that will make guests feel welcomed.

Brainstorm with your team on what might make a great impression on your guests. Bring catalogs full of personalized items such as, candy, coffee mugs, cookies, baskets, tissue paper, cards, and gift certificates to spark some ideas. Better yet, hold a contest among your welcome ministry team members. Give each of them $5.00 or $10.00, a handful of church information and one week. When they return with their gifts the next week, have some impartial judges nearby and a nice prize for the winner. You may not end up using the ideas they come up with, but those ideas may lead you to something else that would work perfectly. You also may be wondering who can spend $10.00 on every guest that comes through the door of the church. Ten dollars allows your team members to buy items the church will be able to buy cheaper in bulk. Also consider how many visitors you host on a weekly basis. If you have one or two visiting families every week or two, maybe you can afford to make a great impression through a gift you give them. If you have 20 guests a week, you may need to keep your gift budget down to a dollar or two per gift.

Another way to make a great impression through gift giving is to display those gifts in a special way. Place a table in your church lobby area covered with a nice tablecloth. Arrange the gifts in an attractive way. Stacking mugs in a pyramid or gift books or tapes in a unique way can really draw the eye of your guest and make a good gift look great. If arranging the gifts is stumping you, start noticing how retailers arrange their products. Gift and bookstores are masters at making their product displays easy on the eyes.

Remember the *personal* touch. A table with well-displayed gifts is nice, but not nearly as nice as a few friendly people stationed at that table. While friendly volunteers give those gifts to guests, they use that encounter as an opportunity to get acquainted with the guest. More important than any coffee mug or gift certificate are the gifts of warm welcomes, sincere interest in the guest, a servant's heart, and going the extra mile. These gifts will make the best impression on your guests. Make sure they are in place first, then a basket of cookies or a sermon tape is an extra WOW and one more way to say, "Welcome."

A table with gifts is not nearly as important as the people stationed at that table.

6. Make the experience memorable.

When it's all said and done, what will your guests remember about their experience at your church? Will they reflect on the cold, standoffish feeling they got when they walked in and no one spoke to them, or will they recall how surprisingly friendly and *real* everyone was? During the drive home will they talk about how your church made them feel like special, valued guests or how they just didn't feel at home? What will they tell their friends and associates on Monday morning about your church?

Part of your challenge in creating "The WOW Factor" is making the guest's experience memorable. Not, "That was the worst church experience of my life!" kind of memorable experience, but the kind of memorable experience that makes her say, "I've never been treated so well in a church in all my entire life!" That's the goal. Tell your welcome team that your goal is for every guest to leave your church actually saying, "WOW" or, "I've never been treated that well in a church," or "I felt so welcome here this morning, let's come back next week." Patients of Dr. Bentham have a memorable experience when they go to him for muffins (I mean dental work). Why? Because he has taken a below average experience and transformed it into something creative, inviting, unexpected, and just plain too good to be true. Ask yourself what kinds of things would have to happen for your guests to leave the parking lot uttering words of excitement and disbelief at how wonderful going to church was. Make a list.

Ask what needs to happen to produce excitement and disbelief.

What needs to happen?
What would that experience look like from start to finish?
What would the memorable highlights of their visit be?

The answers to these simple questions could completely change the way you welcome guests.

Take the "WOW" Challenge

I wish I could be a fly on the office wall of Dr. Bentham's dental experience. I would love to see people pull up to the house and wonder if they were in the right place. "This isn't a dentist's office." Wouldn't it be fun to see their faces when they walk into the kitchen and take the first whiff of fresh-baked muffins? I'd like to watch their eyes get big when they encounter the extra-mile service. There is no doubt in my mind that people leave the good doctor saying, "WOW," out loud. I can hear people talking at work the next day as clearly as if I were in the next cubical, "I have never been to a dentist like this. It was unbelievable." I can hear friends on the phone sharing their experience. "You don't walk into a waiting room, you walk right into the kitchen. That was the best muffin I've ever tasted." Can't you pick up the excitement in their voices as they tell this unbelievable story? Somewhere between dreading their appointment and driving away with a new filling and a bag of muffins, this dentist has created a memorable experience.

If the doc can do it, so can we! If people can get excited over a dentist appointment, we can cause excitement over a memorable, unexpected church experience! Dr. Bentham has given us a challenge. Dentistry is very important. But dentistry isn't nearly as important as Christ. It doesn't even run a close second to spending eternity with God because there is no second to that. Spreading the Word of God and telling your community about the saving power of Jesus Christ is the most important thing you'll ever do. Shouldn't people leave your church saying "WOW"? Take the WOW Challenge! Why should church be boring—something we dread—something that makes guests wish they had stayed home and read the Sunday paper instead? Why shouldn't church be the absolute highlight of your week and the guest's week? Why shouldn't the visitor's experience be worth getting excited about and telling friends about on Monday? With God's power and creative ideas from Him and with a team willing to make the difference, your church can take the WOW Challenge and win. Transform your church into a wowing place! God has big plans for His house and for His people. Ask Him what He has in mind.

Why shouldn't church be the absolute highlight of the week?

Chapter 8

Come On "In"

Helping Guests Feel Like Part of the Church

Maturing from a child to an adult offers us many opportunities for growth. One of those opportunities that seems to follow us from childhood right into our adult lives is how we deal with either being part of the "in crowd" or being on the outside looking in. I remember in grade school certain kids were "in" and others were not. The not so "in" kids weren't chosen for teams or involved in games. In grade school, whether you were "in" or not could turn on a dime. If Joey or Sally said you were "in" on Tuesday, great, you were in! However, Wednesday could find you completely "not in." Sally and Joey could be so fickle! One thing's for sure: kids can be pretty cruel. They point and laugh or they stick out their tongues and make faces at the other kids who aren't "in." In high school being "in" didn't change from day to day. You were consistently "in" or consistently "out." By college, everyone finds their own "in" group and you kind of ignore the other "in" groups. As we get older, we don't point and laugh at people who aren't "in" like we used to do in grade school. Adults don't stick their tongues out at the "not so in" adults. We adults are much more sophisticated in our disregard. We've matured. Adults don't call names and make faces. We simply snub our noses at people who aren't "in." Sometimes we don't even speak to such people; they aren't worth our time.

Surely that doesn't happen in our churches. How easy is your church to "break into?" I'm not talking about picking the lock on the front door. I'm talking about unlocking the relationships that are closed to newcomers. Do the people in your church open their arms to guests and invite them into their circle of friends?

Do the people in your church open their arms to guests and invite them into their circle of friends?

While visiting a young adult Sunday school class, my wife and I discovered how it felt to be outsiders. We walked into a class for younger couples. We had heard the class might match our needs. No one greeted us. We also noticed that everyone in the class had on a special nametag except us, so it wasn't as if it were difficult to tell we were there for the first time. One guy did start a conversation with me, but not a single woman spoke to Amanda. They had snacks and no one asked us to join them. We felt like we were intruding. Surprise! We didn't return for a second visit.

Let's say the Jones family has been attending your church for about a month. If they still feel like visitors, something is very much wrong. At some point, the Jones family, who keeps returning to your church week after week, should begin to feel more and more a part of what's going on. They should begin to feel like they aren't strangers anymore. They should begin to feel like they are "in." I'm not talking about truly assimilating new members into the church. I'm talking about the step *before* the Jones family decides to make a commitment to stay put at your church. Let's call it the "Come on in" stage. Would you like to be part of the solution?

Wouldn't you like to help the Jones family feel that they are finally "in" on things? Here are five "in" words that will help you "in" your quest to bring the Jones family and others inside the circle of your church's fellowship.

Introduce

Matthew 5:47 says, "And if you greet only your brothers, what are you doing more than others? Do not even pagans do that?" Many of us only greet those whom we are familiar with at church. We don't think about greeting the non-Christian or the guest. This passage of Scripture really puts it into perspective for us. We have a responsibility to reach out to those among us who don't know Christ.

When I say, "introduce yourself," I mean spend a few minutes with that new family.

It seems a bit basic to talk about introducing yourself. But when you think about it, introductions these days may consist of first and last names, or they may only go something like, "Bob, this is Mike. Mike—Bob." When I say, "introduce yourself," I mean spend a few minutes with that new family. Learn names. Discover where the children go to school. What does the Mr. do for a living? How about the Mrs.? A great introduction should last five, ten, even fifteen minutes.

This is the point where most of us get nervous. You approach someone new and you introduce yourself, "Hi, I'm So And So." Then, you learn the name of the new acquaintance. Then three seconds quickly tick by on the clock and you have forgotten the name of the person you just met. Do you have trouble remembering names? Lots of people do. However, these same people that cannot remember names can recite their social security number on command. They know their address, their phone number, their pager number, their cell phone number, their spouse's social security number. They could sing phone numbers of all their friends to the tune of "The Star Spangled Banner," but they cannot recall the person's name to whom they were just introduced.

Why? For me the answer is simple. When I forget a person's name within the same, short conversation in which I first learned it, somewhere in the back of my mind I've told myself that I'll never use his name again. I remember all my own personal numbers and the numbers of all my friends because I use them on a regular basis. If, while I'm meeting someone for the first time, I just repeat to myself, "I am going to need to remember Mark Smith's name. I am going to use Mark Smith's name again," then I'll do much better at remembering his name. In fact, I think I'll use Mark's name in the very next sentence I speak in my conversation with Mark. "Where do you work, Mark?"

Another great way to remember names is to imagine something funny or crazy in your mind, linking their names with their faces. For example, when I first met Mark Smith, I noticed that he had a really big forehead. (I picked this feature because I share the same big forehead plight, as our imaginary friend, Mark.) So, I pictured using a big black MARKer (note the use of Mark's first name) and writing SMITH right across his forehead. Now I've linked Mark's face with his name. Experiment with whatever works for you. Just picture how pleasantly surprised Mark will be next time I meet him and I walk up to him and confidently say, "Good morning Mark! How are you on this beautiful Sunday? Are Julie and little Sarah with you this morning?" By remembering Mark's name I communicate to him that I am sincerely interested in him. That's our next "in" word: interested.

Interested

The guests you introduce yourself to need to know that you're interested in them. You don't prove that by telling them, "Hey Jones family, I'm really interested in you!" You prove that you're interested in the Jones family by asking questions about them and listening to what they have to say. Ask about their work, their children,

You prove that you're interested by asking questions and listening.

what brought them to your church. Find out about their church experience so far. Have they been looking at churches for some time? Are they new in town and were actively involved at the church they attended in their last hometown? Ask about their hobbies and their interests.

The key here isn't just to *act* interested in them, but to *be* interested in them. Before you approach the visiting family, ask yourself why you want to get to know them. Remind yourself that God brought them to your church for a reason. You may be part of that reason. Perhaps God is planning to bless you with a new friend or with an opportunity to really minister to this particular family. Pray about your encounter with the guests. Ask God to use you to help them feel more at home at your church. Ask God to open their hearts to your effort to get to know them. Ask God to give you the resources you need to answer questions or help with concerns they might have about the church.

What if you haven't quite yet won the battle of remembering names and details about the people you meet? This Sunday after you talk with the guests, go home and write down their names, their children's names, their hobbies, and what they do for a living. Review that information before you get out of your car next Sunday morning and be ready to jump back into a conversation with them.

Invest

Investing in your newfound friends goes hand in hand with being interested in them. Let's say over the last two or three weeks you and the Jones family have really hit it off. You've talked with them every Sunday. It seems that each week your conversations become a bit more natural, and you've really learned some interesting things about them. The Jones family recently relocated from the Midwest. They've been settled in for about three months and have just now started looking around for a church home. Rob Jones is the new American History teacher and coaches the golf program at the local high school. His wife Sharon is a pharmacist and loves to go to theater productions. They have two boys, Steven, age 8, and John, age 6. Both of the boys are in soccer programs. You take the step of investing in your new friends when you decide to use that information to build a relationship with them. Maybe your wife loves theater, too. I'll bet they could talk about the shows they have seen and would love to see. As they grow closer, they might even plan to see a show together or you might make a couple's evening out of it and have dinner together before the show. You happen also to love golf and you read a great article in a golf magazine the other day. You decided to clip it out and give it to Rob. It turns out to be a great conversation piece. As far as the kids go, you have a baby girl, no little soccer players, but that doesn't mean if your family and the Jones family hit it off, you wouldn't find yourself at a soccer game now and then.

Making an investment in lives requires time and effort, but the payoff is worth it.

Making an investment in the lives of the guests in your church or a particular family that God draws you to will require some time and a bit of effort, but the payoff is worth it. In fact, doesn't that scenario on interest and investment that I just described sound more like what the church should be rather than bumping into people week after week and only having a few exchanged good morning's to show for it? Paul said in 1 Thessalonians 2:8, "We loved you so much that we were delighted to share with you not only the gospel of God but our lives as well." What do you think that Scripture means? I think it's talking about investment. Who better to invest in than people that God brings to your church doorstep who are looking for a place to belong, for a place to share their lives with others who love God and want to grow closer to Him. They may not share their life story the first time you talk with them, and if *you* do, they may not want to talk to you again, but over time, as you learn what God is doing in their lives, you may find a true blessing from investing in them. Who knows, you may find that God uses them to make a difference in your own life.

Invite

So often we invite acquaintances to a church event or program, and even as we speak the very words, we realize we're not all that sincere and they are probably not going to show up. Don't just invite for inviting's sake. I remember when I was in junior high and our youth group would host a special event. With all the determination and zeal of an Olympic tournament my friends and I would compete to see how many people we could invite to the event. We would race from friend to friend at school inviting them to our spiritual shindig and then move right on to the next person, mentally checking them off our list. Was there anything really wrong with a competition like that? Probably not. Was it terribly effective? Certainly not. Our best results occurred when we invited people with whom we had built relationships. When the people we invited could see that we sincerely cared about them and really wanted them to come to the event because we knew it would add to their lives, they were more willing to respond. Don't invite someone to a church event just because it's the Christian thing to do. Before you invite, ask yourself, "Am I willing to follow up with these people? Am I willing to talk to them if they actually come? Would I ask them to sit with me during the program or would they be on their own while I sat with friends?" It all boils down to whether or not you're willing to invest in the ones you invite.

Don't invite someone to a church event just because it's the Christian thing to do.

Inviting the Jones family to the church Christmas craft fair and dinner theater is a great way to spend time with them and get to know them. In most cases it's probably easier to invite a guest to a church program than it is to go to a movie or to a ball game with them at first. Church is a good, familiar, common-ground kind of place for your families to interact and get acquainted. What's that? You say your church doesn't have very many events to which you can invite friends or get to know recent guests? Why not make one up?

Invite guests you want to get to know better to a "Preacher's Pizza Parlor" at your church. The preacher hosts this event at the church. Two or three families form a team and each team has a variety of ingredients at their disposal to create the perfect pizza. As the teams make their pizzas together, families become acquainted and have lots of fun. The pizzas are baked and then judged by the preacher in categories of taste, appearance, design, team spirit, etc. Every team ends up winning a prize for a different reason. Everyone enjoys the pizza buffet afterward.

Organize a church talent night complete with drinks and desserts. Instead of sitting on pews in the auditorium or rows of chairs in the fellowship hall use round tables or borrow card tables to make the seating arrangement more relational and warm. Build plenty of time into the program to get to know the others at your table.

Host a "People in the Pew" party at your home. Invite several couples from the church along with several new guest couples. Ask get-to-know-you questions and go around the room learning about each person. Ask questions like:

"What was your most embarrassing moment?"
"When you were a kid, what did you want to be when you grew up?"
"Where in the world would you most like to visit and why?"
"If you could go back and change one thing in your life, what would it be?"

Allow plenty of time for casual conversation over dinner or snacks.

It's not what you do that's important; it's that you do *something*! Do something that will get people together in a fun and light atmosphere that gives them a chance to get to know one another and have fun with "church people"—seeing them outside the context of their Sunday best and the typical rush-in/rush-out church service.

It's not what you do that's important; it's that you do something!

Involve

After you've built some rapport and a foundational friendship with the Jones family, a logical next step is to involve them. Maybe you have similar interests and similar gifts. Perhaps they could join you in the ministry area where you volunteer. Is there a special need or special project coming up in your church? Ask that new friend to team up with you and others to accomplish the task. A simple, "Hey, Rob, the leaders asked me to repaint one of the classrooms at church." You don't have to sign the Jones family up for a five-year ministry commitment to get them involved. Try starting out with some little projects. Your request might be something as simple as these: "Hey, Rob, the church leaders asked me to repaint one of the classrooms at church. Would you like to help me one night next week?" or "Sharon, I am going to be bringing cookies to VBS one night this week, would you like to come over and help me bake, and we can take them to the church together and help serve them to the kids?"

You might find that involving the Jones family at church gives you a great opportunity to jump-start your own involvement. Maybe your church has a list of different ways of getting involved or projects that need to be tackled around the church. Why not display those opportunities on a bulletin board and categorize them in groups like: "Family Project," "A 2-Family Project," "Projects for 3 Married Couples," and so on. People in your church can sign up for the project that's most appealing to them and take the information right off the bulletin board.

Most of us want to be a part of something bigger than ourselves.

Sometimes we shy away from asking people to get involved. We hesitate to ask for commitment. Just remember that most of us want to be a part of something bigger than ourselves. We want to be "IN." If the guests who come to your church stay guests and never build a relationship with others, and don't find a way to get involved, they will not hang around long. The relationships that we form and the roles that we fill bind us to the organizations we come in contact with. The church is a little different. In the church those relationships and those roles are built on and focused on Christ. What a great difference!

The "In Crowd" Should Expand!

There's nothing wrong with your church having an "In Crowd" as long as that "In Crowd" is constantly expanding. If your church's "In Crowd" hasn't changed much in the last six months or the last six years, it's time to take some action. A small "In Crowd" of people who are "in" on everything and involved in everything and who do everything must turn a corner and begin involving more and more of those churchgoers who are on the outskirts of involvement. A "Card-Carrying In-Crowd Members Only" mentality won't cut it. If that attitude continues, the church may dwindle down to consist only of that small, closed "In Crowd" and no more. Instead, church leaders should strive to encourage and empower the "In Crowd" to seek out others and involve them.

Open your eyes to those on the outside looking in.

"My church isn't very welcoming to guests. My church doesn't get people involved," you say? *You* are the church. Open your eyes to those around you who are on the outside looking in. Open your mouth and say a kind word and get to know the people you've been sitting behind every week in services. Open your heart and build a relationship or two. Open your will to God and allow Him to use you to make the difference to a guest who really wants to be part of the family.

How would you feel if you were treated like a guest in your own home? I know, you're thinking, "Pretty good. That sounds like a pretty easy life." Maybe so, but you would never really feel at home. Imagine people constantly taking your coat and asking you if you'd like something to drink. Imagine those same people keeping you in the front living room (the clean part of the house) and never letting you see the basement or the closets or the little nooks and crannies that every house has. What would it be like to always be spoken to in smiling small-talk chatter? You couldn't relax. You would never feel really at home. Would it even be home? There are certain experiences that are part of being a family, aren't there? You share in the chores and projects. You can discuss all kinds of issues without worrying about how it sounds. You can help yourself to the "fridge." You can stretch out on the couch. You can take your shoes off and kick back and relax. You are home. There's a comfort to knowing that you belong in a place. You're "in." At some point the guests of our church would like to make the transition from guest to part of the family.

How many people in your church right now are on the fringe? Either they are new or they've been guests for weeks and weeks. Maybe they've been uninvolved for years and years. I'm sure they would like to be part of the family. I'm sure they'd like to share in the to-do lists and in the joys and sorrows that every church family shares. They probably have a few joys and sorrows of their own to share with you. Help them feel at home. Connect with them. *Introduce* yourself, show *interest* in them, *invest* in their lives, *invite* them and *involve* them. After all, every Christian has been adopted into the family of God. Someone took the time to introduce us to Jesus. He was interested in us enough to leave Heaven and come to earth to show us how to live. He invested in our lives by giving up His own and shedding His blood for us. He invited us to come and lay our sins and our worries at His feet. Jesus involved us in the process of showing His love to others.

Shouldn't we say to our guests what we want Christ to say to us?

One day we will stand at the doorway of Heaven and all of us will hope to hear those words, "Well done, good and faithful servant. Come on in." Those might be the best three words in the history of words. Don't you think it's time we say them a lot more in our churches through transforming outsiders into insiders? "Come on in."

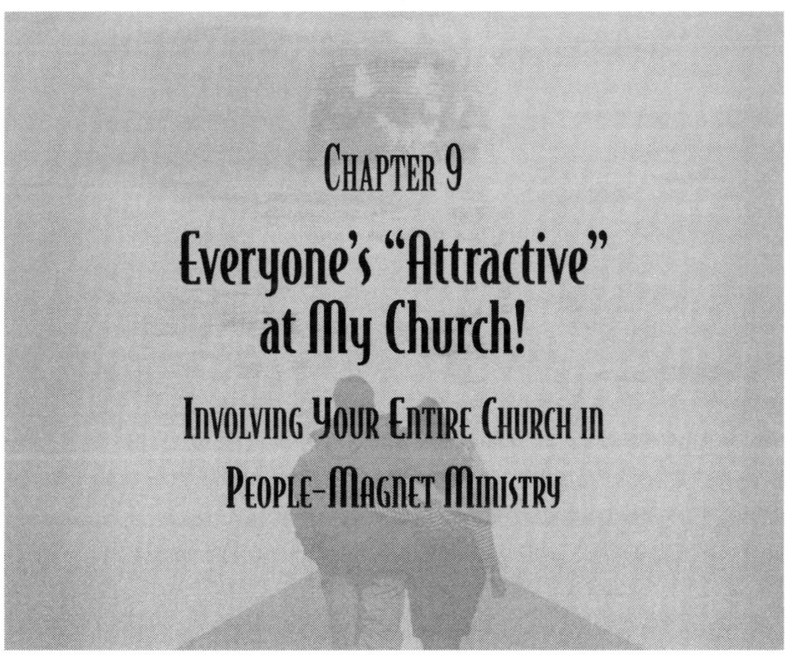

Chapter 9

Everyone's "Attractive" at My Church!

Involving Your Entire Church in People-Magnet Ministry

Magnetizing Your Church

Maybe you feel as though you are the only person in your entire church who is passionate about making the church a friendly and welcoming place. Odds are very good that you are not alone. Most everyone knows what it's like to have been treated less than warmly. We've all gotten the "You're not welcome here" feeling before. Having those kinds of experiences, coupled with a passion for reaching people with the love of Jesus Christ motivates us to transform our churches into people magnets. Do not despair. You are not the lone magnet at First Community Church of Scowlville. There *is* a remnant! So how do you resurrect that remnant? How do

You are not the lone magnet at First Community Church of Scowlville. There IS a remnant!

you encourage, exhort, nudge, or just plain shove your church into the world of welcome? Let's look at a few ways God might choose to stir up your church. That's an important point. Let's put first things first. God is the power behind this endeavor. The steps I offer are not part of a magic formula but merely suggestions. Acknowledge that if God doesn't work in and through you and others, there is no way you can accomplish these goals. Pray to Him. Call on Him. Ask Him to transform the hearts of the people in your church. Ask God to provide key people to be involved in this ministry. Pray for a spirit of joy, welcoming, and care for the people God sends your way to sweep through your church!

Creating a Culture

Churches don't go from being people repellent to people magnetic overnight. The transition takes time. A culture of friendliness and genuine joy and care must be created. Culture, simply put, is an environment or a climate. Create an attitude among the people of your church that encourages friendliness toward everyone and eagerness to meet guests and make them feel at home. Somewhere along the line your congregation must understand that being friendly, joyful, sincere, and welcoming isn't something we *do* occasionally, or even something that we're *in the habit of doing*. It is ***who we are*** as a church.

Make It a Value

Make being a People-magnet Church one of your church's values. Many churches have listed their core values in addition to wording a mission statement. Core values might include, "People matter to God, and therefore they matter to us." "The Bible is the Word of God and must be proclaimed boldly!" "Prayer is powerful. We desire to fuel this church through the power of Prayer." Or, "We are a People-magnet Church, drawing people to Jesus Christ through loving and serving them in a Christlike way."

If your church values being a People-magnet Church, the specifics of what everyone should do to help make that happen should be always before the congregation. Provide the congregation with reminders. Use posters or bulletin boards, articles in church newsletters, and biblical application supporting the effort in messages from the pulpit. In short, make the expectation clear. In creative ways let the congregation know that there is an expectation of friendliness and sincere warmth. This is not just one person's job or just a ministry team's job. It is the job of everyone who is a part of your fellowship.

Model the Desired Result

If you don't know where to begin in this journey, or if you've tried creating a culture and communicating a value and it's gone over like Aunt Ruth's Split Pea Layer Cake at a church potluck, try modeling the desired result.

Assemble the movers and shakers of the church: ministry staff, the preacher, elders, deacons, church leaders, Sunday school teachers, etc. Make an agreement to model people-magnet behavior. Decide that your group is going to turn the tide in the church. You're going to spread joy and smiles and a servant's attitude throughout your church at every opportunity.

But what if you're not a church leader or the preacher or a Sunday school teacher? Remind yourself that you and God make a great team. Commit to making this your personal mission. See if you can make a difference in three or four weekends at your church!

You can either be a thermometer or a thermostat.

I heard it explained this way, "You can either be a thermometer or a thermostat." When you walk into a room do you mirror its mood and attitude like a thermometer would mirror a room's temperature? Or do you ***set*** the temperature in a room like a thermostat? When you walk into the room, do the moods and attitudes brighten up a few degrees? That's the goal. You effect a change among the people around you and among those who come in contact with you on Sunday morning.

Reward the Excellent

Every church has one or two or twenty people who are natural people magnets. These folks greet people without being asked to do so. They smile and laugh. Nothing energizes them like talking to perfect strangers. Build up these people! Mention them by name as you're explaining to the congregation the friendliness and warmth you want your church to be categorized by. Maybe you're not into publicly recognizing people. No problem; reward them privately. Call your church's group of people magnets into a leader's meeting and present them each with a smile award. Send them personal notes telling how much you appreciate their joyful spirit, that you've noticed how they lift the spirits of the congregation and how they go out of their way to welcome people they haven't met yet. Pick up the phone right now and call some people magnets and encourage them. Thank them. Tell them you're going to begin to pray that God would multiply ther spirit among the people of the church. We'll talk about how to get these folks actually involved in your welcoming ministry later, but for now let's start with an easy one: reward, uplift and encourage the people magnets of your church!

Maybe you're not into publicly recognizing people. No problem; reward them privately.

Celebrate the Difference

As your church begins to develop into a people-magnet church you should notice some changes. The difference may be subtle at first. Maybe you notice people sticking around longer after the services are over. Perhaps the greeting time in your church will become livelier. You may even see more and more people talking with guests. Praise God! While you're at it, praise the congregation too. Preacher, a quick word at the conclusion of the service every so often could reinforce the positive things that are happening. You might say, "I just want you to know that I have really noticed a difference around here lately. More people are smiling and getting to know one another and welcoming our guests. That's awesome! God will do amazing things as we continue to invest in people and show one another the love of Christ." Why not encourage the congregation? Why not let them know you can see a difference? Let them know that their ministering to one another will make a difference for eternity!

Beginning a Welcome Ministry

Okay, so you don't have an official welcome ministry at your church. How do you start one? It can go by many different names. Greeter Ministry, Hospitality Ministry, Welcome Ministry, Guest Services Ministry, to name a few, or maybe you have a new clever name in mind to add to the list. The goal is for your church to become *intentional* about becoming a people-magnet church. God can take our small efforts and multiply them into big results. No matter what size your congregation is, you don't need an army to start a welcome ministry. You just need to start one!

You don't need an army to start a welcome ministry.

Just as we talked about at the beginning of this chapter, don't make a move until you pray about this. Ask God for His guidance as you look into starting this ministry. Don't just ask God to bless what you're going to do, ask Him to show you what to do and how to do it.

After you've prayed about the possibilities, your next step will be to share your passion with the church leaders. If you are a member of the church, you'll need support and help from the leaders, preacher, or another member of the ministry staff. If you're on staff at the church, you'll need the leaders to join you in this goal. If you're a church leader, you'll need consensus among the other leaders on the team and staff. As you informally discuss your thoughts and ideas with the appropriate people, share with them a basic plan and some of the goals you think are important to achieve. Assure them that you are willing to commit and willing to help or lead in any way they think would be beneficial to the church. It also wouldn't hurt to let them know you understand you don't have all the answers and you'll need their help and support but mostly their prayers. Pray together before the meeting is over.

Go on a Smile Hunt

Once the green light is shining, go on a smile hunt. "What's a smile hunt?" you're asking. Well, it is what it sounds like. You will need a perceptive set of eyes and ears. In order to be an expert smile hunter, start noticing the friendly people at your church. I am sure that you can name a few right now. If not, this whole challenge just became even more important! Picture those friendly people in your mind. What makes them so likable? They are positive and joyful. They have a good, outgoing personality. Maybe they smile a lot and seek out people to get to know or encourage. Scout them out a little bit this Sunday. Start noticing who the most friendly and upbeat people are in your church. When you get home, make a list and start praying.

Start noticing who the most friendly and upbeat people are in your church.

After you've observed for one to three weeks, make a list and pray over that list. You're ready for the next step—approaching the friendly people on your list.

Invite Them on the Journey

Don't be anxious about asking the people you nabbed on your smile hunt to join you on this journey of ministry. Look at it like this, at *least* these people are friendly. They probably won't call you bad names or punch you in the stomach or walk away and never speak to you again. However, they may decline with a very friendly smile. Positive, outgoing, friendly people are usually busy people. Do you know why? Because they're people magnets, that's why. People are drawn to them, and they are drawn to people and may be involved in lots of projects in and outside of church. If they say no, then thank them, tell them to keep the ministry in mind and in prayer. Remember, you're praying God would lead you to the right core of people to begin this important ministry. Trust Him to send you the very best magnets for His glory. When you approach someone with this challenge, explain what you'd like him to be involved in.

Positive, outgoing, friendly people are usually busy people, because they're people magnets.

You might say, "Jeff, God has really given me a passion to begin a welcome ministry in our church. A ministry that would go out of its way to make the church a more friendly place and to give our guests a special warm welcome." Next, let Jeff know why you're talking to him. "I have been noticing how outgoing and friendly you are. You really have a God-given gift for making people feel at ease and at home. You're exactly the kind of person this ministry needs." Then, give Jeff a chance to pray about it and let him know you'll be talking to him again. "Would you pray this week about being involved? And would it be OK with you if I talk to you again about it next Sunday, or maybe give you a call later this week?" That's basically it. Jeff may be so excited that he signs up right away.

"I've been praying about this very thing and I would love to be part of the team!" he may say. But, he may need to pray about it and ask some questions. "I will pray about that and give it some thought. What kind of time commitment are you thinking this will require?" Or, as we've said, Jeff may just say no right away. "I would love to, but I'm a little overcommitted now. Would you keep me in mind a little further into the process?" Maybe he will want to jump on board after the ministry takes off and the congregation begins to see the difference.

When you've made it around to everyone on your list, you'll discover what kind of core team you have to work with. Don't be discouraged if you only have a few people on the team (counting yourself)! Three passionate and dedicated people on the team are better than 25 who are half-hearted and playing along out of guilt or obligation. Take what God gives you and run with them. Think of your core team as the loaves and fishes and watch God multiply the ministry!

Set a date and hold your first get-together. Before you do, make sure you invite the congregation. Inform them that a core group of people interested in making the church a more friendly and welcoming place will be having an information party. Let them know that if they love people, smile a lot, and want to see the church grow, God may be calling them to give a new ministry a try!

Make It Fun

There are some ministries of the church that are very necessary but not necessarily fun. Ministering to the sick and grieving is a must. It's a command. But it's not very fun.

People should think, "This is going to be fun!"

Welcome ministry is *fun*. Make sure your first meeting (did I say "meeting"? I meant party) is fun (and every get-together thereafter). When people walk into this information party, they should be pleasantly surprised and should think, "This is going to be fun!"

There are lots of great supplies on the market these days. Go to your local party store or discount department store and pick up some smiley-face plates, napkins and yellow tablecloths. How about using yellow smiley-face balloons to fill the room? Throw some colorful candy around the meeting table. Order a cake or some cookies iced in the smiley-face theme. Go all out! If you want to WOW your guests, start by *wowing* the people who will serve them. Whether this is the first welcome ministry meeting in your church's history or your church already has greeters, ushers, and welcome center volunteers who just need a nudge of excitement, this fun setting will get lots of laughs, smiles, and comments.

Cast the Vision

At your first party, don't get bogged down in a bunch of business and detail. Cast the vision. Motivate. Excite.

Explain how a welcome ministry could make an eternal difference in the life of a guest. Your team's friendliness and willingness to serve could be what makes guests return to the church a second, third, and fourth time. If they return enough and they see enough of Jesus Christ, they will fall in love with Him and give Him their hearts. Let your core volunteers know that this could be one of the most important ministries in the entire church! Make this a time of excitement and exciting prayer. Ask God to bless your church through this ministry in ways you never dreamed. Ask Him to start the blessing this Sunday!

For your first week just ask people to show up at church 30-40 minutes before the worship service. Have the team meet at the appointed time at a special spot. This is your opportunity to pray together before you serve, and for the leader to renew the vision for the ministry. Then ask them to select a door to greet at. If someone is already at one door when they arrive, ask them to find another, or to select a place in the hallway or lobby area. Ask your core group to pray every day at a specific time about this ministry. Hand out a reminder prayer card that they can put on their fridge or in their car. Ask the team to pray for God to use them this Sunday as they greet and welcome and serve. Then, set a time to meet again after Sunday and let them know you want to hear all about their first experience serving as a greeter. Maybe next Sunday night they could come over to your home, or you could meet again at church. Aren't you eager to see what God will do?

The Next Level

After you hear how God blesses the team and you see how a new spirit of friendliness and service blesses the entire church, you'll want to move to the next level. Schedule greeters to a specific door or area each week. If you have enough, you may want to rotate volunteers so that a greeter serves every other week or every other month. Why not have a welcome ministry party about once each month? The party celebrates what God is doing in your church through the welcome ministry. It also gives the team a chance to discuss ideas about how to improve the ministry and go the extra mile for the guest. You may eventually want to have nametags made for the greeters and other welcome ministry volunteers. Consider using a yellow smiley sticker or a colorful nametag to set them apart and make them recognizable to the guest who may have a question or concern.

It's Not Rocket Science... It's Heart Surgery!

Don't try to make this ministry hard. It isn't. It's not rocket science . . . it's heart surgery! It doesn't have to be complicated. Instead, focus on people's hearts; warm up their hearts. Put their hearts at ease when they walk in the doors of your church. Make their hearts smile.

Don't try to make this ministry hard.

Help to organize, support, and encourage the people in this ministry area. Other than that, let them loose to welcome and WOW. Continually remind them why they do what they do. It's easy to become complacent and think, "I'm only handing out a bulletin." "I'm just guarding a door." "I just stand here and say good morning about 1,000 times." No, no, no! You're in the people business. Not the bulletin business. Not the door business. Not the repeating words business. You are in the *people* business. You are in the same business as God! Always keep telling the people involved in your ministry that what they are doing has eternal consequences.

If I Be Lifted Up

Jesus made an awesome statement in John 12:32. "But I, when I am lifted up from the earth, will draw all men to myself." Jesus was and is a people magnet. He, more than any idea or method discussed in this resource, will draw people to Himself. I believe with all my heart that it is our responsibility to communicate the story of Jesus to a lost world in the most creative, clever, and unique ways possible. I believe we should use every resource, medium, talent, and gift available to us to make a connection between those in our communities and Jesus Christ. But, I also believe that none of those methods will be successful unless we realize one very important spiritual truth: Jesus is the Divine Magnet. We are not the true magnets. Our ideas and methods are not the magnet. Our creativity and cleverness have no pull without the power of our Savior Jesus Christ.

Much as the opposite poles of magnets are attracted to one another, the opposite characteristics of Jesus Christ and those of sinful men and women pull us to Him. Not because He needs us and we need Him, but simply because—we need Him. Jesus is pure; we need to be purified. Jesus is righteous; we are seldom right, but often sinful. Jesus is holy; we are full of holes. Because of our desperate need for a Savior, He draws us to Himself. Aren't you thankful that God didn't wait for us to find Him? He sent Jesus, the one-Man search party, to seek and save the lost. Once you meet Him, once you learn of Him, you will fall in love with Him. Your soul will be magnetized by your need for grace and forgiveness and peace and living hope. Then, "click," like two magnets snapping together, you will stick to Jesus. You will cling to the Savior. Jesus is the ultimate people magnet.

Why Is He So Magnetic?

Jesus was speaking in reference to the cross when He said those words, "when I am lifted up from the earth, I will draw all men to myself." Jesus' words were brought to life as the cross He was nailed to was lifted into the air and dropped into place. In that awful moment of torture, the unmistakable reality of God's amazing grace toward us is made known. There is also a vivid illustration to be seen of who Jesus is. Picture the scene as if you were watching from a distance. Christ was lifted above the ground of Golgotha, suspended between earth and Heaven. Our Savior was suspended between God and man. I see that as a perfect snapshot of His life and purpose, because He was God's appointed middleman. *The* go-between. First Timothy 2:5 puts it this way, "For there is one God and one mediator between God and men, the man Christ Jesus." Jesus Christ is the only one *able* to stand in the presence of God on our behalf, and the only one *willing* to leave the presence of God to die on our behalf. Isn't He the most magnetic personality you've ever encountered?

When I get to heaven (because Jesus was willing to be my go-between), I want to talk with Job. The first thing I ask Job will not be about his suffering. I won't even ask about his faithfulness in the midst of tragedy. The first thing I will ask Job is, "Tell me the story of when you first arrived in Heaven and saw Jesus Christ for the first time." I imagine that it was an awesome sight. Why would I want to hear specifically about Job's first encounter with Christ? Because Job begged God for a go-between, he basically hoped for Jesus Christ. Job 9:33 records his request, "If only there were someone to arbitrate between us, to lay his hand upon us both." Job wanted someone who could put one hand on God and the other hand on man. He asked for someone who could represent God in the flesh, yet identify with man and our frailty. Job didn't get his request granted at the time, but our eternity and our today is forever changed because God already had such an arbiter in mind. After Job relates his first encounter with Christ, the one he prayed for, I'm going to tell him, "Even though Christ's coming to earth was planned long before you made the request, thanks for asking." Jesus is the people magnet of all time. He fulfills our deepest and most critical needs. He places one nail-scarred hand on God and the other nail-scarred hand on us.

Job wanted someone who could put one hand on God and the other hand on man.

No amount of strategy or cutting-edge methodology could take the place of the power of Jesus Christ—His life, His sacrifice, His call on our lives. Our churches must lift up Christ in exaltation. They must lift Him up by preaching the power of His story from the pulpits. They must lift Him up by sharing the amazing story of amazing grace. Our lives must lift up Christ by following His example. By living life and loving people the way He lived and loved. No church can be a people magnet church without the divine people magnet, Jesus Christ, as the centerpiece and focal point of all they do. Let's study some principles and examples from the life of Christ that will help us match our approach to drawing people to that of our Lord.

A Love for People

Jesus showed us how to *love people*. Jesus loved people regardless of their station in life. Regardless of who they were or who they were not, Jesus loved them. Jesus loved people who could not repay Him because they had nothing. Jesus loved people who were resistant toward Him, even those who wanted Him dead. Jesus loved sinners who were ashamed of what they had done and those who were proud and defiant. Jesus loved people deeply because He could see deeply into their hearts and souls. He knew what was missing in their lives. He knew He could fill their emptiness. Jesus loved the people that everyone else ignored, avoided, and shunned. Jesus looked at those who were diseased and demented and disgusting and demon possessed, and He loved them.

What would happen in your church next Sunday morning if the kinds of people Jesus loved walked in and sat on the front row? One by one they walk down the center aisle: prostitutes, robbers, cheats, liars, adulterers, murderers, and plainly despicable people. What would the reaction be? Remember, if we want our churches to be people-magnet churches, we don't get to pick the people, God does. What if this were the group God sent to your church? Would they be spoken to, welcomed, embraced? I'm not sure most churches would pass such a test.

What would happen in your church next Sunday morning if the kinds of people Jesus loved walked in and sat on the front row?

If Jesus personally led a church today, His church would respond with love. After the benediction the people would model the actions of their Shepherd. Instead of heading in the opposite direction of the motley group of sinners on the front row, the church would flock down to the front to meet the guests. Warm words of welcome, smiles, and laughter would only be interrupted by sincere discussions and prayers shared between the faithful and those in need of faith. I would imagine there would be some hearty handshakes and hugs offered in humility. Relationship foundations would be built. The newcomers, with all of their sins and shortcomings, would feel like they had found a family and a place where they now belonged. They would begin to see that unconditional love is not just a concept found only on bumper stickers and in catchy Christian phrases. They would discover it is a characteristic embodied by Christ and His people.

Before we go any further, just be reminded that prostitutes, robbers, cheats, liars, adulterers, murderers, and plainly despicable people do walk down the aisles and hallways of your church every single weekend. We have all sold ourselves to sin, giving away who we are, and whose we are, for pennies. We have all stolen from God what is rightfully His: our loyalty, worship, and love. We have cheated our friends and family and neighbors out of the joy of knowing Christ because we are afraid to bring Him up in conversation. We have all lied to God and ourselves. We have all committed adultery by giving ourselves to the world instead of to the God we promised ourselves to. We have all murdered by gossiping or hating or holding grudges. We are all plainly despicable people. But we are all forgiven by the blood of Christ. Praise God, He didn't demand that we pay for our crimes, but sent His perfect Son to die in our place. What if God were to look at the front row of your church next week and see the types of people I have described? Then if He were to look at the second row, full of senior saints, church leaders, and faithful Christians, the only difference would be that one row had experienced God's grace and the other was about to have same the opportunity.

A "While Others" Approach

Jesus had a "while others" approach to ministering to people.

While others threw stones, He forgave.
While others avoided sinners, He attended their parties.

While others made rules to rule over people, He placed people before the rules.

While others built walls, He made a path.

While others slept, He prayed.

While others counted change, He multiplied lunch.

While others said, "No more allowed!" He said, "Let them come."

While others walked away, He ran toward.

While others didn't want to be infected, He touched and healed.

While others said, "It's over," He said, "Remove the stone."

While others said, "His ministry was just beginning," He said, "It is finished."

While others grimaced, He laughed.

While others were calloused, He cried.

While others said, "There is no way," He said, "I am the Way."

While others judged, He cleansed the record.

While others were selfish, He gave.

While others said, "You don't belong," He said, "You've come to the right place."

Is your church part of the *others*? Or is your church on the side of the unexpected, full-of-surprises Savior of the world? When guests come to your church do people avoid each other, throw stones, and build walls? I pray they forgive, embrace, welcome, and tear down barriers. When the visitor takes a chance and reluctantly gives church a try, do the people at your church say, "You don't belong. No more allowed!" or do they say, "Come on in; you've come to the right place"?

If Jesus personally led a congregation today, His church would respond differently from the others. When the guests expected the door slammed in their faces, Jesus' church would fling the doors wide open. When the guests expected the people of the church to treat them like outsiders, Jesus' church

Jesus' church would fling the doors wide open.

would treat them like long-lost family. When the guests expected church to be awkward, cold, and stiff, Jesus' church would be lively, warm, and loving. If Jesus were CEO of a church today, the guests would find there the most challenging of calls, the most joyful of spirits, and the most sincere of hearts.

A Meeter of Needs & *NEEDS*

Jesus met needs. He met everyday "needs," and He met eternal, spiritual "***needs***." He talked with the woman at the well and gave her everyday respect and then gave her eternal freedom. He attended a wedding reception and gave the host everyday wine and a not-so-everyday miracle for guests to remember the occasion. He fed the 5,000 an everyday meal and gave them a spiritual lesson. He went boating with some fisherman, performed their routine job with not so routine results, then netted some disciples who then caught the eternal vision. He saved a woman from her everyday life and from being stoned and, in the process, gave her eternal hope. Jesus met the everyday, common needs of people: food, water, conversation, and help. But He didn't stop there. He also provided their spiritual and eternal needs: forgiveness, hope, peace, healing, love, significance, and belonging.

Your church can provide both as well. It can be a place where people are treated well. Your church can be a place where they are given the basic needs of companionship, purpose, relationships, and conversation. It can also, by God's power and the ministry of the Holy Spirit, be a place where they can receive instruction, encouragement, and the unsearchable riches of Christ.

If Jesus personally led a congregation, it would be a place where both *everyday* needs and *eternal* needs were met. Each person would get the individual attention and love he craved. It would be a place where everyone that made up the church family would share with one another and encourage newcomers and charter members alike to continue to grow in the grace and knowledge of God.

It's Not out of Reach

If Jesus personally led a congregation, it would be a church of unconditional love. Everyone would be welcomed, and everyone would be loved. It would be a people-magnet church. It wouldn't follow what others said or did. Instead, while others ignored, crossed arms, or walked away, it would embrace with open arms and open heart. It would be a people-magnet church. It would be a church that met needs. It would be a church where everyday and eternal needs were met. It would be a people-magnet church.

If Jesus personally led a congregation, it would be a church of unconditional love.

Here's the ironic, but good news. *Jesus* ***does*** *lead the church.* Jesus *does* oversee and guide and lead and run the church! The church is *His*—His bride, His body, His redeemed children. A people-magnet church, where Jesus is in charge and where people are drawn to Him is not out of reach; it is within our grasp. It is a question of surrender to Him. It is a question of abandoning yesterday and pleading with God to show us a way *today* to reach our communities for Jesus Christ.

The exciting part is that, although Jesus could do it all by Himself, He chooses to allow *us* to be part of this awesome project—saving the world. He allows us to participate, surrendering/*returning* our God-given gifts and talents, and offering our resources and our hearts. In a million different ways, He gently reminds us that He is to be our focus, our purpose, our source, our goal, our reason, our aim, our destination, our redeemer, and the lover of our souls.

> *Now to him who is able to do immeasurably more than all we ask or imagine, according to his power that is at work within us, to him be glory in the church and in Christ Jesus throughout all generations, for ever and ever! Amen.*

Suggested Reading and Resources

Connellan, Tom. *Inside the Magic Kingdom: Seven Keys to Disney's Success.* Staten Island, NY: Bard Press, 1997.

Freiberg, Kevin and Jackie. *Nuts!* New York: Broadway Books, 1996.

Toler, Stan and Alan Nelson. *The Five-Star Church: Transforming Your Church with Jesus' Model of Servanthood.* Ventura, CA: Gospel Light, 1999

Willingham, Ron. *Hey, I'm the Customer: Front-Line Tips for Providing Superior Customer Service.* Paramus, NJ: Prentice Hall, 1992.

Direct Mail

Manlove Church Marketing
1107 Center St., Pasadena, TX 77506
www.churchmarketing.com

TV Commercials

M-Pact Productions
3939 S. Harvard Ave., Tulsa, OK 74135
1-800-422-7863
www.impactproductions.org

New Resident Addresses

New-Pro's Data Inc.
740 Lakeview Plaza, Suite B, Worthington, OH 43085
1-800-937-5478

About the Author

Darren Walter is currently the Guest Services Minister at Southeast Christian Church in Louisville, Kentucky. Southeast averages over 14,000 in attendance each weekend and continues to grow with God's blessing. The Guest Services Ministry is made up of more than 1,400 volunteers actively serving in the Greeter, Usher, Communion Preparation and Serving, Section Host, Welcome Center, Tour Guide, and Guest Reception Ministries.

Darren holds a Bachelor of Arts degree in Bible and Ministry with an emphasis in preaching from Kentucky Christian College, where he and his wife Amanda met. In addition to his ministry at Southeast, Darren enjoys presenting seminars and training sessions at churches around the country, on various subjects including becoming a visitor-friendly church. Amanda's ministry, Dramatically Different, brings a unique touch to church programs using her talents in drama and music, specializing in women's events. For more information on either of these ministries, check out Darren & Amanda's Web sites:
www.dramaticallydifferent.com and www.magnetministries.com

In addition to *The People-Magnet Church* Darren has authored articles for Christian publications and coauthored a book with his close friend Scott Tucker entitled *Follow Me Again* available now through Covenant Publishing.

Taking Out the Garbage
Leaving Your Past
Ross Brodfuehrer
We accumulate so much "garbage" inside of us. Fortunately it is never too late to get rid of it, through the power of Christ. Pure and holy living is possible even in this day and age. This wonderful study is set up on a daily basis for your group members, with discussion questions that will work well in a weekly small group setting. In their efforts to live a life that honors God, your group members will find this study helpful and encouraging.
89 Pages, soft, $7.99

Charting Your Course
Directions for Real Life
Ross Brodfuehrer
Ever feel like your spiritual life was drifting? It doesn't have to be that way. This study will help you and your small group members get back on track. This practical and valuable study will guide your group members to a renewed, vibrant walk with the Lord. This helpful resource is set up for daily study by your group members, and allows for weekly small group discussion and questions. Your group will appreciate the fresh relationship with Christ this study will help create.
115 Pages, soft, $7.99

Controlling Your Pests
Ridding Your Life of Bad Habits
Ross Brodfuehrer
Like nagging insects, bad habits continue to afflict your life. Despite trying to drive them off, they continue to buzz about making you conscious of their presence. This helpful study will help you and your group members understand that there is relief available. You will discover ways to bring those pesky habits under control. This resource is designed for daily study by your group members, and is suitable for weekly discussion and interaction within a small group environment.
115 Pages, soft, $7.99

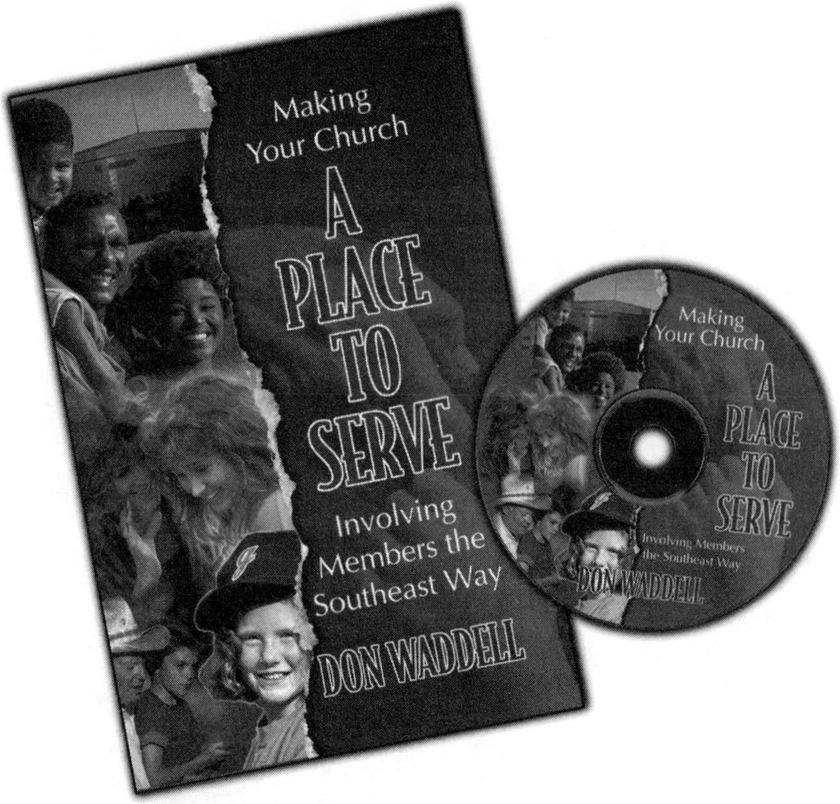

MAKING YOUR CHURCH A PLACE TO SERV

INVOLVING MEMBERS THE SOUTHEAST WAY

DON WADDELL

The statistics are staggering. Thom Rainer in his book *High Expectatic* found that if members of a church only attend worship services, only 1(will still be attending in five years. If however they become an active p of a Sunday School, that percentage goes up to 83%.

Southeast Christian Church does not claim to have all the answers, a this is not a magic book of formulas, plans, programs, or gimmic Rather it defines a process toward inviting people to an intimate relatic ship with God. The CD contains 200 pages of letters, phone scripts, b letin inserts, applications, etc., which are being used in the ministry Southeast Christian Church. When you purchase the CD, you have p mission(see copyright conditions on pages 8 and 44 of the book), to ref mat and reprint this material to fit your church needs. This is an excell resource and will be a great help in the ministry of your church.

160 pages, soft, reg. Price $10.99
CD (appendix), reg. Price $6.99